LOVE FALLS UP

Six Silly, Sly and Surprising Stories

LOVE
FALLS

UP

Six Silly, Sly and Surprising Stories

Julie Prentice

PRENTICE
PUBLISHING

VERMONT

TO ALL QUORANS

CONTENTS

AUTHOR'S ACKNOWLEDGEMENTS

"Alice laughed. 'There's no use trying,' she said. 'One can't believe impossible things.'

'I daresay you haven't had much practice,' said the Queen. 'When I was your age, I always did it for half-an-hour a day. Why, sometimes I've believed as many as six impossible things before breakfast.'"

Lewis Carroll, *Alice in Wonderland*

A WORD (OR TWO) ((OR THREE)) ABOUT ME

Hi there! My first fiction readers. Welcome! Thank you so much for supporting me by buying a copy of my book. Electronic or physical (either way) we are good.

I hope these stories entertain, engross, and enthrall you. If you fall asleep or hate something, let me know. I promise to read every email. Although I can't promise to write back to each and every one of you, I will do my level best to answer 99.99%.

Email me at **prentice.julie.e@gmail.com**.

Email **lovefallsup@gmail.com** to join the fun and sign up for my mailing list.

Email **hey@julieprentice.com** for information about a rare, in-person or Skype interview.

Visit **julieprentice.com** for more special offers

and deals (you awesome reader!).

Like you, I like stories. I think of myself as an avid reader with a good imagination. I like to get lost in other people's lives, walk for awhile in their shoes, view the world through their eyes, and sit for a while with their friends.

I started writing at a very early age, starting with a diary and the idea that I should write things down lest they be forgotten. One day (at age five), my mom was tucking me into bed; she whispered, as I was closing my eyes, that she wished she had kept a diary—to better remember her life.

Memory is an elusive and intangible thing. Some incidents remain permanently within easy reaching distance. These accessible memories are conveniently brought into the forefront by daily activities, sights, sounds and smells. Others remain elusive and, even in dreams, seem veiled and cloudy.

It is indeed amazing for me to reread entries in my diary that I made five, ten years ago and view them with objective eyes.

There are numerous things that seemed so important to me then that I was compelled to write them down on paper. But I would have forgotten those incidents entirely if I had not written them in the pages of my pink diary (a hand-me-down from one of my older sisters).

You guys should try this; I promise you will have

fun. And learn about your life and the people you love.

I envied my sister her diary, and, when it fell into my hands one day (before it became mine), I defaced it and scribbled in the pages. I don't remember if that is how I ended up with it (or if she simply grew out of it) but, a year or two later, it became mine.

Your diary can be locked up; the key hidden; its pages plumbed by only the owner. This really intrigued and emboldened me. My diary safely stored thoughts and feelings that I usually kept under lock and key. Wait...it was still locked, but, at least, no longer just inside my head.

The ability to write things down, to tell my secrets to an impartial and sympathetic ear, helped me to make sense of some of my crushes.

I was too shy to share my crushes with my friends or sisters...sometimes, it is even too embarrassing to think back and remember some of them. You know?

My diary made me think about what I truly wanted in life and to write down my innermost doubts about things I was taught, especially from my religion teachers. I got in the habit of writing things down at an early age. This habit has stayed with me, like a beloved beauty freckle, all the way into adulthood.

And, I hope, eternally.

Writing, to me, is almost a game. Think of a scene! Put some characters in it! Then, let your imagination hold your hand and take you away on a new adventure.

These little vignettes are little ellipses in time, little episodes that I romanticize in my head and allow myself to daydream about. More often than not, these episodes are inspired by good movies I've seen or books I've read that challenge me to think about someone else for a little while; to view the world with a different perspective for an hour or two. Or five or six or a lot more for a long novel.

I love to people watch and sometimes I make up a quick story in my head about how that person's day has gone before I saw him or her. Who are the smiling (or frowning) eyes as he or she opens the door; how many pets come running to him or her?

The whole enchilada.

An idea for a story can hit me out of the blue and I am compelled to write it down (if you are so inclined, give it a try, too).

Or, it can be an idea for a scene that plays out in my head like a movie. Other times, my writing is more contemplative; I put some effort into what I want to say and how I'm going to say it.

I really like Cecilia Ahern's writing style. Magical realism. Remember oxymorons from the English grammar class you slept through? You wakefully slept through the magical realism unit.

In writing assignments for school, I would start with a more fantastical version of the story than I eventually handed in. My parents and older sisters ably edited. But, I would usually change the story before showing it to them. My original drafts were often too outlandish to be read by even them.

As time passed, I began to stick to the rules of the assignments decreed by benign dictators (otherwise known as my teachers).

I found other outlets to express my creativity. I started to write novels, poems and short stories.

My first novel—*Living Through the Years*—is unfinished, but, I started writing it on one of our rare Snow Days (when you live in Vermont, schools and everything usually stay open when it snows) while Bing Crosby sang, "White Christmas" on my Walkman (and, yes, I still have that Walkman ;).

I followed that story with another "novel" that I called, *The Time Mix Up*. It, too, remains unfinished, but it started a trend. A personality quiz I took resulted in the letters ISFP (Introverted, Sensing, Feeling, Perceiving). Apparently, it is a weakness of my personality type to start many projects and have difficulty finishing them (I'll keep working on that; promise :).

My time became more structured (you guys can relate?) as I got older, however, and even writing daily in my diary became too hard to keep up. Don't be stressed if you try writing in a diary and find the same thing happening to you. There are years that have been neglected in my diary (little summaries being the most I could handle).

And then I started to write a third novel. Untitled.

Still unfinished. I started the "novel" my Sophomore year and continued to work on it up until my Senior year, during free moments when I wasn't otherwise doing homework, reading a book or eating lunch. I only finished about ten single spaced pages of the "novel", but the thrill of having a secret novel, of writing something that nobody else knew about, helped me to steer through long days of sports' practices and intense (chase the good grades) studying.

It was my secret; it was liberating. I was a novelist! Maybe even a paperback author! Someday...

The act of writing has kept me alive, joyful and full of wonder. To be able to turn a blank page into a page full of a story, my story, with characters that I alone can name, kill off and mess with, is an amazing accomplishment.

Words have the power to create new worlds and possessing the ability to enter a new world—albeit for only a short time—is exceedingly important. And very cool. Yes. Very cool. :)

Now: follow me down this very silly, very sly and very surprising word journey.

My stories are now your stories.

Our stories.

Yours From (Snowy) Vermont,
Julie Prentice

PART I

LOVE

"...And now these three remain: faith, hope and love.

But the greatest of these is love."

1 Corinthians, 13:13.

Spaced Out

"Just love her." I picked up my plastic spoon and swished it through my peppermint tea.

"What does that **mean**?" He quizzed.

"It means...you know..."

"No, I don't know."

"Yeah, you do. It means love her in such a way that she feels it. I mean really feels it. Deep down."

At that moment, I suddenly succumbed to the urge to use my hands to demonstrate. I made a serious face—eternal love conquers all—and pressed my hands close to my heart, willing him to understand my intense belief about "deep down." He sneezed.

"I have absolutely no idea what you are talking about. Unless you are referring to sex in some way." He took a sip of his own coffee; black.

"No! I'm not talking about sex!"

Men!

"Then what? You are not making any sense."

"I don't know how else to explain it."

I was flabbergasted; how could he not understand? It is so simple. Heartfelt; that's a word for a reason, right?

"Try. No, forget 'try,' just explain it." He really sounded mean, didn't he? But, his tone was conversational.

"OK, I'm going to have to use a story; I really can't explain it any other way."

"You are wearing my patience. Fine. Just keep it relatively short? Please?" Mean squared. Or raised to infinity.

"You are an absolute asshole sometimes, you know that? Why am I even friends with you? And I'm not "wearing" anything. It's wearying."

I really hate him sometimes. He can be such a complete and utter arrogant fool. I wonder what he thinks of me.

"Whatever. I don't know. Explain, please." That wasn't an apology. Not even close.

I sighed. "Fuck. OK, fine."

"OK, start. Now."

"Be quiet and I will."

"OK."

"OK. The story goes like this...shit." I looked up and immediately turned away from the door, hoping against hope that I wasn't seen. George looked at me like I was nuts.

"What? Shit? That makes even less sense."

"No, stupid head, 'shit' my ex-boyfriend just walked in."

I quickly ducked my head again and prayed for MR. FUCKER! to miss me; I don't know how I ever dated him. I must have been high. Or maybe just deranged. Or both. Luckily, he didn't appear to see me, or, if he did, he ignored me, too. MR. FUCKER!

"Ignore him. Continue, please." Why did I even sit there, taking that?

"Do you even hear yourself?"

"Yes. I said, 'Ignore him. Continue, please.' I said, 'please.'"

"Like that makes it all better."

"Doesn't it?" How he pulled off a naif-like innocent expression, I'll never know.

"No!"

"How about now? Are you ignoring him yet?"

"You are too much!" If I were the type of person to throw my hands in the air, stand up on the table and shout this, I would have. As it is, I just glared.

I really don't know how he made it through middle school. Or High School. Or two days.

"I don't know if you are being sarcastic right now. Please just tell the fucking story." He said this with a smile that magically erased the sting out of his swearing. But, still. We don't need to use "fuck" every time we speak.

"Leave out the "fucking" next time and see how that works for you."

If voices could demonstrate a second eye-roll, mine would have echoed my eyes perfectly.

"Please just tell the story." He smiled at me, batting his eyelashes in an attempt to fake a ditsy act.

"You really are something." But, really, I couldn't stop a smile from invading my eyes and the corners of my red (some have told me they are luscious) lips (OK, it was one old boyfriend; that was my favorite thing he used to say, "You have such red, luscious lips"). He's George. Exasperating, but still endearing. Sometimes.

"Is that a good thing or bad thing?" George has a hard time understanding what I say. Or what anyone says.

"Who knows, at this point." I sighed.

He stared at me with a blank face, as blank as a document taunting a brilliant work of creative fiction.

"I'm ready for the story. Have you got it?" How did he do that? Have absolutely no clue that steam was literally coming out of my ears?

"Maybe. First, would you tell me why you even talk to me?" Because, goodness knows, it is a real mystery. One of the biggest mysteries of all time. Bigger even than who helped the mummies create their pyramids. Or something. Before they became mummies. You know what I mean. It was aliens, of course. Right? Or time traveling westerners. Either/or. Maybe both.

"Yes, OK, later. I will. I will tell you that. Yes. Now, you tell the story." He put his hand over his mouth and impolitely burped loudly right into it. I just stared. And honestly couldn't think of what to say next. He was asking me for an impossible feat; to get a girl to like him. Strike that. Spend more than two seconds with him.

"Why? Why do you need me to tell you so badly?" I swallowed hard. He had nothing to say for a beat. I waited.

"Because I want to get her...how do you say? I want to get inside of her...her pants and her brain."

"Dude. You're going to have to tone that way down. She is not going to like that." What in the world was he thinking?? Her pants and her brain??

"I dunno how to say it."

"That's the best thing you have said all afternoon." Sheesh.

"Thank you." His face looked smug.

Ugh! Must remember not to give him any compliments. They go to his head.

"How did you meet her again?" How he did not

hear my incredulity is another mystery. At this point, I wondered if she were even real.

He scratched his chin. It looked like he couldn't remember; either that or he just really didn't want to tell me. It's probably something extremely embarrassing. Like a chat room for My Little Pony fanatics. Ha ha!

"I mean, how did you get her to start talking to you?"

"I hit her."

"What the fuck??!"

"Hit on her."

"Ha ha ha ha. You did??"

"Yes. I hit on her."

"How?" Ha ha ha; I really couldn't stop laughing. It's really comical. George's game. I couldn't even imagine it.

"Frankly, I was just hitting. I do not remember. Tell the story. I feel that she and I will have sex at least two times due to emotions."

"What the fuck!?! Dude, you need to stop talking like that!"

"Like what?" True expression of confusion permeated his pretty face.

"You're hopeless." Face palm.

"I'm not."

"Yes, you are. How the fuck have I never heard you talk about girls like this before?"

"I dunno." He looked blank again. How does he do that?

"What do we usually talk about?"

"Computers."

Ahh, techies.

"What?" He took a napkin off the table and squished it into a ball in his hand.

"Nothing." I cleared my throat.

"What??" He looked cute then, scared.

"You wouldn't get it."

"Get what?"

"Exactly."

"You aren't being clear. Just tell the fucking, I mean...just tell the story. Please. Now."

"Fine." I sighed. He did try to leave out "fucking" that time.

"OK. And...go."

To tell the story with a modicum of context, I have to start at the beginning. You just met me and my Computer Science (CS) pal, George. He's...George; I don't know how else to describe him. He's unlike anyone you've ever met; or, if you have met him, you wrote him off as an asshole and forgot you ever met him. Or, if you remembered, you designated him as "That Ass" and forevermore associate donkeys, evil masterminds, and George in the same umbrella in your mind (just be careful not to use that umbrella in the monsoon season; it will undoubtedly have a hole in the middle, drenching you at the most inopportune time).

By the way, I'm Natalie Silver. And George's surname is Lopez.

We were having coffee in Starbucks, which, let's face it, has become THE IN place to hang out. Bars make you feel guilty, especially if you are a programmer and have no game whatsoever and can't reasonably order a cold one at 3:00 in the afternoon.

Bars and daytime equal a bad combo. The wood reeks, the room itself feels tiny and musty. The blinds have to be drawn because bars are nocturnal. Neon lights and sunlight don't mix well, just sayin' (unlike a smooth Vodka and a delicious tonic).

George had just met a girl. But, not any girl, THE GIRL. The one who made his heart pound. At least, during that particular phase in his life. And, depending on how receptive THAT GIRL is for you, she can end up being THE ONE. If she agrees, of course.

He was asking me for help and he seriously needed it. Did you hear him? Unbelievable. But true. He said those things. I am his witness. He actually said, "I think we could have sex at least two times due to emotions."

I mean, really. George! Get fucking real!

Unfortunately, I was distracted. An ex that I never wanted to bump into again, literally or figuratively, had walked in when I was going to recount my own past love history for George, thereby definitively answering all his universal questions about love, women, and relationships.

I was a fool. But, he was a bigger fool for believing that my pearls of wisdom on the subject would apply to THE GIRL (that's beside the point).

I was rudely interrupted and had a hard time focusing on the conversation once THE EX FROM HELL walked in. Seriously. No. SERIOUSLY. And, I'm not joking. But, I, Natalie (sometimes Nat) powered through.

If you were confused, about our prior conversation and who was talking, etc., I really am sorry, but I was too lazy to put in any setting or "he saids" or "she saids" or "I replieds" consistently.

Sometimes, telling a story is like working in a Bangladeshi retail factory of an American corporation. Hard work! You're welcome. I am doing all of this hard work for your benefit. So, again, you're welcome.

Wondering when this story gets good? Don't worry, it's about to. Read on.

And dream on.

"OK, you have to love her. You have to find out what makes her tick. You have to study her, like you've never studied any subject before in your life. And, you have to use every single trick in the book to pull this off."

I took a break to sip my peppermint tea. My George took the opportunity to mirror me and sip his black Colombian roast.

He finished his sip and then unnecessarily said, "Which book?" *Major face palm.* I kept my head down like a downward facing dog in a YMCA yoga class. I really wanted to teach that boy about how real people talk. Another time. I delved deep inside for patience and inner calm. Poise. Ommmm...

"Find out her likes, dislikes. Habits. Hobbies. Activities. Basically, everything that makes her *her*. You need to do all of this background research and really be a stalker. Be her biggest stalker. Just, not a creepy one."

He stared at me. He had a look on his face that every programmer sees in the mirror after writing, "Hello, World!"

"I'm kidding about the stalker thing. That was a joke. You were supposed to laugh."

He just looked at me. His eyes shone. "No, that wasn't a joke, Nat."

"Yes, it was."

"Nope."

"Yes."

"Nope."

"You're going to be her stalker?" Shudder. Was he serious?

"Yes. I already am."

"What??!"

"Ha. Ha. Ha ha ha. Joke!"

"I'm going to kill you." Lightning shot from my eyes. If only.

"Ha. Ha ha." He has a very annoying laugh. Let me just tell you that. Very. Annoying.

"I really hate you right now."

"OK. Ha ha."

Grrr!!!!

"Ha ha ha ha. OK. Tell me something practical. This is a waste of time."

I was stunned into silence for a half a beat.

"Just forget the whole thing!" I really don't know why I even bother to talk to George. Ugh!

"What?"

What do you mean, what???

"I said, forget it!" I wanted to slap him. Again. "It won't work." I sighed, resigned. "You are too unromantic."

"That's crap. All that romanticism stuff is complete bullshit."

"That's what *you* think."

"Psychology, psychobabble—it's all crap someone invented to make money." The scary thing is, he really believes himself. And only himself.

"And diamonds are all a marketing scam," I said, making no effort to conceal my sweet sarcasm.

"Exactly." Sarcasm is wasted on George. As would be a good wine. I'll keep both to myself.

"Yup. Just forget it."

"Why?"

"You aren't fit for the dating world. Just hire a prostitute. Or, better yet, have an arranged marriage or get a mail-order bride. I give up on you." I mean, really. *I feel we will have sex two times due to emotions! WTF!*

"I do hire prostitutes." How did I forget who I was talking to? Lord. "But, she isn't one. If she were, that would be so simple. I could just offer her money."

"There are no words."

How could he look so nonchalant? Did he actually believe this crap??

"I really have no words, George."

"I doubt that. You talk too much."

!!!!!

"Fine. You're right. I was being polite." I smiled like the Cheshire Cat, if the Cheshire Cat's smile were closer to the grimace of the insane Joker (played by Jack Nicholson) from one of the Batman movies.

"I know."

"OK, here's my advice. Don't open your mouth. Ever. Don't say a thing. The only way you will get her is if she never hears you speak. Ever. Just smile. Pretend you're a mute. That should do it."

He smiled at me. I gave him a thumbs up. "That's perfect; just like that. If she doesn't fall in love with your looks, then opening your mouth is going to drive her away faster than...faster than that avalanche can cover you."

"What avalanche?"

"The avalanche advancing toward you."

"There is no avalanche."

!!!!

"It's a metaphor—just forget it."

"You're the one who brought it up."

I wish he would think before he opened that cute mouth of his.

I glared.

I thought for a second, then blurted out, "47."

We both laughed.

Quick background: 47 is our own version of "42."

42 is The answer. THE answer. To life, the universe and everything (as seen in "A Hitchhiker's Guide to the Galaxy").

Then I had an *Aha!* moment. "I've just figured it out, George. You're a number and the rest of us are letters. Not meant to be mixed."

"What about x and y?"

"You know what I mean..." Damn his quick mind.

"Do I?"

"Yes. You do."

"OK."

I looked up at the room and then quickly back at George, my pulse racing.

"I need a favor." My voice sounded breathless, my breaths sped up in only a second.

"Ask."

"Can you kiss me?" I was almost frantic.

"When?"

"Now!"

I didn't wait; I leaned, shifted my weight downward, pressed firmly over the table between us and forced his head to mine, our lips mashing together.

George's mouth was open to talk, so my lips met his tongue. I gasped involuntarily and this resulted in George's tongue in my mouth.

Our eyes were still open. His brown eyes were wide and confused like an innocent child's. My blue eyes exuded panic much like some teenage girl being chased by the masked killer in a slasher/horror film.

I quickly shut my eyes and mustered strength to focus, as if George weren't George...as if he were George Clooney and this kiss were the only chance I would ever have with George Clooney. Sigh.

I opened my right eye again, ruining the illusion,

and checked; phew, my ex had seen us lip-locking and was turning away. Yes, keep turning, MR. FUCKER, keep going!!! You don't want to see this. I closed my eyes again and put both hands on George's face so he couldn't go anywhere or pull back. I opened my eye just a crack again and the coast was clear. Yes! I stopped kissing George as quickly as I had begun, releasing his face and sitting back in my chair again.

"Can you pass the napkins?" I shifted my voice, adding in an extremely nonchalant inflection, pretending none of what had just happened actually took place.

George blinked. Ooh. His face. Priceless!

"Uh…" His voice was husky and he had to clear his throat. Lol.

"The napkins? Thanks." I fought back a smile as he found one and passed it to me. His hands were shaking. It was so delicious…his discomfiture. It radiated off of him like a woman's excess perfume trapped in an elevator. He cleared his throat again. I concentrated on my napkin. I kept my face down so he couldn't see me trying hard not to laugh. My panic vanished as soon as THE FUCKER had slithered away. Starbucks snake.

"What, um, what, why…what was that?"

"What was what?" I played dumb blonde; *My George's* favorite game to play with *me*.

"That, the err, kiss?"

"Oh, that!" I made my voice sound like it had been nothing.

"Yes, that."

"Just seeing something."

"You…what?" His face!!! I mean, totally and ridiculously priceless.

"An experiment." I faked nonchalance again. Hmm.

I'm pretty good at acting! Maybe I could start a new career...

"An experiment." He repeated me. He sounded so confused. I laughed gleefully in my head. "And...?" He looked at me expectantly. Expecting what, though?

"Nothing." I said, making sure my voice communicated my frivolous disrespect. Ha! Maybe I really could be an actress!

When I looked up at George, dejection had thoroughly invaded his face.

Oops. Did he want me to *like* that kiss? What???? No, we are JUST friends. He can't possibly want sex from me. Or, actually, he's a guy. So, he probably does. Definitely.

"You just saved me. Err, both of us, actually." I quickly explained.

He really did. That kiss kept THE FUCKER away; it would not have been pretty if he had tried to talk to me.

"How? What's going on, Nat?" Now he sounded worried. Maybe he thought I had gone off the deep end. But he wouldn't have thought that. He would have just thought that I was crazy.

"My ex, remember?"

"Yeah?"

"My Dark Ages? *THE FUCKER*??"

He nodded. I continued.

"He was here. Evil enters Starbucks."

"Where? Where is he?" Now he was just playing dumb again. He looked over his shoulder and scanned the café.

"He's gone now."

"Phew."

"Yeah, tell me about it. Thus, the kiss."

"Oh."

I could tell that he was running through some of the more unpleasant memories from that time in my past; I had called on him a lot during the *after-THE FUCKER phase*. Or maybe he was thinking about the kiss again. I thought of our kiss. I suddenly felt the urge to wipe off my face with every napkin on the table.

They don't tell you, those Romantic Comedies, they don't tell you that kissing isn't the wonderful, amorous, heart-warming lip-lock depicted on the silver screen.

Kissing is wet. And messy. It's not all that pleasant. It makes your lips, chin and the top of your mouth all wet, as if you tried to chug warm soda and missed, getting it all over your face.

Kissing makes you want to wipe your mouth off, but, you can't really do that without seeming rude. Or, if you're still kissing, his mouth gets in the way of your hand and he's just going to get it wet again, soon, anyway. Breathing and swallowing become awkward. You think about how you are now swallowing his saliva and breathing in his carbon dioxide. So, in actual fact, kissing is like putting the bottom half of your face in a bowl full of warm goo, swallowing some, and seeing how long you can hold your breath before you pull your face away.

Add to the mix a weird, wet, warm, tongue muscle that feels like a huge slug pushed in your mouth, too. Then swirl it around. Inexpertly.

If you are not kissing someone you like 100%, the hormones that should be released like adrenaline and oxytocin—the little helpers who make kissing bearable and even surprisingly enjoyable—are absent. Face in a bowl of warm George goo plus inexpert slug.

Yikes!

Luckily, we were in a Starbucks and I could take a sip of my delicious peppermint tea to wash out the lingering Colombian roast taste in my mouth mixed with George's saliva. And then wipe my face on a napkin.

I should probably stop thinking about saliva and slugs before I get too grossed out.

The portrayal on screen is not the reality. Those actors and actresses deserve Oscars just for repeatedly kissing their coworkers, surrounded by tons of people, sweating profusely under hot lights, wearing dense makeup like foundation, eye-shadow and lipstick, that's simultaneously rubbing off and getting eaten. Yeah.

Bet you never thought of it quite like that before.

Kissing someone you like, on the other hand, can be great; but you have to have the butterflies in your stomach that make it worth the slobber and oxygen deprivation. Not to mention the pimples that can show up on your face from repeated make-out sessions clogging your pores with a combination of your saliva mixed together.

Kissing George was odd.

We'd been friends for too long. Any sex fantasies I had about George occurred before he started talking and ruining his chances with me. Permanently.

But, he's still my friend. And, more than that, one of my best friends. Gah. That's sad. I must make a New Year's resolution to find new friends. But, he did save me from THE FUCKER. He's not all bad.

"You owe me one, now." He looked smug.

Scratch that. Arrogant bastard.

"I do not!" I had no trouble voicing my disdain. "That was for your benefit, too."

I took a breath. "I just gave you your first kiss." I

smiled. "You should be thanking me." Ha ha.

"Very funny."

"I thought so." Ha ha ha.

I looked up again and stopped laughing abruptly. A pair of eyes met mine. Gorgeous eyes. Magnetizing. Invigorating. Possibility swam in his eyes, and beckoned, "Come with me on an adventure. You won't regret it."

Intriguing.

The rest of him was quite average; a little taller than the average Joe, black hair, black eyes, tan complexion and a typical business suit outfit, probably Brooks Brothers. But, I'm not a connoisseur of men's fashion, so I have no idea if that's accurate.

George and I were dressed casually in comparison; George in jeans and a t-shirt, plus sandals and I was in my standard v-neck t-shirt plus crystal covered fun jeans and comfy Mary Janes. It suddenly seemed like I should be wearing something else. Something fancy. Or, at least, fancy undies. Mine were gray cotton.

I didn't realize how preoccupied I had been with Mr. Gorgeous Eyes until George practically shouted my name.

"Nat! Earth to Nat!"

Rather, nickname. I jumped like I had been scalded by his black coffee.

"Sorry!"

"Are you here?"

"Nope. Not really." I grinned. I felt like a sheep. "Don't look now, don't look! There's a gorgeous guy over there."

"Where? Gorgeous guy?? I don't see one. They all look pretty average to me." He mumbled the last bit, but not quite softly enough for me to miss it. Was his tone a bit petulant?

"Is he still looking at me?" I felt nervous, jumpy.

"I dunno."

I looked up again and saw him type something into his phone. He looked up afterward and into my eyes. Whoo, boy. Definite tingles went up my spine, as if I had caught a sudden draft. I turned back to George with some effort.

"He's waiting in line. He's in a navy suit with a striped tie." Yummy. He looked good enough to eat in that suit. I wouldn't mind a slobbery, oxygen deprived slug match with him!

I took another sip of my tea to have something to do. It was almost out. Only one or two sips left. I made a quick decision.

"I'm going to get a refill. Want anything?"

"Nah. Wait, yeah. Get me a cinnamon bun."

My mouth watered just hearing those words. Yum! But so off limits.

"'K."

"Oh, and ask for extra frosting." Double yum! Why did George have to torture me like that?

"Sure."

I got up and moved to the back of the line; Mr. Gorgeous eyes watched me walk (I think) because I felt his eyes on me. You know how that happens sometimes? You can just tell? He watched me. I stood a few customers behind him. This was strategic...if he got a coffee, I would be able to learn his name. Then I could cyber-stalk him. Hee hee. I looked at the display case; cinnamon buns! They looked so good!

George and I definitely share a sweet tooth. I think that's part of why we are such good friends. He likes my baking. Also, he orders the dessert I'm too chicken to and then I get to taste a few bites, unless I'm being super good (and worshiping the paleo, low-carb gods) and abstaining. Cinnamon bun with *extra* frosting. Double yum.

So, now, you're probably at the edge of your seat. Right? Right? Exactly. Now you're wondering: what's up with me and George? Do we get it on? Do we get together? Or, do I do the "girl" thing and go after another guy even though I have the perfect "best friend" in front of my nose?

Exactly. Edge of your seat. I knew it.

But, of course, there's more to the story.

I took my own ill advised advice I gave George and started e-stalking Mr. Gorgeous Eyes. I found his name and profiles online and Googled him extensively. Did you know that you can get some real dirt on people using Google? Like, old high school photos (shhh...don't tell anyone). And maybe it would be a good idea to start using an alias at places like Starbucks. It's shockingly easy to learn someone's name.

And, the more I found out, the more I fantasized about him. Ooh...he's on Pinterest? What Pins did he make this week? He's on Facebook? What does he share with the public? LinkedIn? Twitter? Skype? What other internet social media sites does he have?

But, after getting my e-stalk fix, I would inevitably head to my new favorite site, an off shoot of Quora, kind of, and kind of like that Ask Me Anything page from Reddit.

It's so cool. It's an app on Facebook; you get recommended by your Friends to answer questions. It's totally addictive. It's called Ask A Friend.

Once you start getting more and more points on your answers, they get more widely distributed. Points are the whole point (pun intended, ha!). You can use them for anything; Amazon Prime takes them,

Marriott Rewards takes them, Mileage Plus takes them...they're awesome! And all of the points come from your answers—if people "like" them or not.

Okay, there are also some more details to the points thing, and it's calibrated by some special algorithm and it's based on your reputation and how you answer and, basically, you can't give points to your friends for a crap answer and then get points from them in an endless loop.

You actually have to answer well. People can post comments on your answers and can offer feedback, as well. And...this is where the site gets tricky. All comments are anonymous. On the one hand, this is cool; if I want to give a scathing comment to a dear friend of mine and don't want them to know it's me, I can. Yay! However, it also means I can't see who are giving the scathing comments to me.

And I have an Anon who keeps targeting me.

He's the most zealous, nit-picky, anal retentive Anon ever. He has to be male; he can't be anything but. He drives me insane. I've only ever seen him on my answers (of course). Leave it to me to get stalked by a Grammar Nazi.

However, he does so much more than pick on my syntax and paragraph organization. He's on every single one of my answers (and answers that get tons of points!).

On the one hand, the attention is flattering (who has the time to go through all of my answers with a fine tooth comb?). He must actually, secretly, really really like me. I hope. If not, I've made one very obsessed cyber enemy. Well, at least, a cordial one. Because all Anon comments have to be strictly cordial and academically relevant to the answer. Otherwise, it gets deleted by the moderators. The moderators remind me of Donald Sutherland in *The Hunger Games*.

About a week after the George kiss in Starbucks, I logged on and discovered my answer for—*How do you choose men?*—had gotten 10 points (yes!) and, again, one comment at the bottom.

Here we go...

Anonymous: *Your first sentence ends with an ellipsis which is not necessary to establish your point. You can use a period instead of a semi-colon in almost all of your sentences. Anyone speaking this answer aloud would have no time to take a breath. Essentially, your entire answer is comprised of run-on sentences. As to the content in this particular answer, I have only one comment: You should let them choose you, instead.*

OH DEAR GOD!

The nerve of this Anon! What the fuck???

Obviously, his last dig was missed by the moderators because his comment was mostly about punctuation. Unless...he is a...gasp!...moderator, and is able to post on all my answers regardless of what he says.

Abuse your power much, Anon???

I had to call George and tell him about this new affront; I call him whenever a particular comment gets my goat. He's great at telling me to shut up and stop thinking about a stupid online persona. That whatever Anon says is meaningless. That he's just doing it because he can and that I shouldn't waste any of my thoughts on him. Of course, I secretly wonder if George just wants me to shut up about Ask A Friend altogether. Hmm...must find a way to get this answer from him. I should probably just ask point blank. He will have no compunction against telling me exactly what he thinks.

"Hello?" George sounded utterly flummoxed, like he had no idea who was on the phone. Didn't he know that it was me? I was calling on my cell phone to his cell phone...he must have seen my name pop up. That's what caller ID *is*. Sigh.

"Hey, George!"

"Let me guess...Ask A Friend guy strikes again?"

"How the hell did you know that?" My jaw dropped. Though, he couldn't see me, so why I bothered to do that is beyond me.

"I finally made an account. It's much faster to read about it than to hear everything from you on the phone."

"Oh. You really want to read all of it?" Total waste of his time; he must be joking. Wow, I really do use semi-colons a lot.

"No, I just saw your most recent answer and his comment." George sounded kind of bored.

I sighed. Audibly. "George," I whined, "why is he doing this to me?"

"He must be in love with you. There's no other explanation." George started to laugh. His voice sounded kind of tinny on the phone; his laugh is much better in person. Unless it's his annoying laugh. Then it's worse.

"Well, now that you've got an account, do your computer voodoo and see if you can find out who he is for me."

George is a genius at computers; I'm only a novice. I ask him everything because I don't know anything. He always has a great answer. He's also great at retrieving information; I think he's a closet Hacker...he must be. The things he knows are just too good to be true.

If anyone can find out who Anon guy is, George can.

"Why would I waste my time doing that?" Great; all of my hopes, dashed. Just like that.

"Because you're my super duper best friend in the whole wide world?"

"Try again."

Argh!

"Because...you like me to bits and pieces?"

"Not funny. You're no bit." I think George is smiling on the other side. But I can't be sure.

"Ha ha ha. Okay—I've got it. Because, otherwise, I'll bore you to tears talking about Anon guy every day for the rest of time."

Silence on the other end.

"You would do that." He sounded resigned. Yes! I had him.

"You know me!" I sang down the line.

"Fine. I'll do what I can. Much easier than dealing with this drama all the time." Success!

"Thanks, George! You're the best." I was practically leaping with glee.

"Yeah, yeah."

"I'll bake you something awesome when you're done."

"Bearclaws?"

"Sure!"

What's a bearclaw??

Little did I know that this very conversation would come back to bite me—big time. But, who can predict the future? No, there's no such thing as a crystal ball. However, I'm kind of convinced by the Psychic Twins; they seem to be able to predict all kinds of things. Maybe I should have asked them. But, I didn't. Naturally.

I sprinted to the Starbucks from my apartment, totally energized by my success on the phone with George. I ordered a non-fat latte and added in a vanilla cake bite (to take the sting out of the most recent Anon comment). Coffee smells so good. Its aroma always makes me feel like I'm in heaven: safe, warm and happy. It's the best smell. If there were a coffee perfume, I'd wear it, just to smell it on myself all day long.

Glorious.

Anyway, who did I bump into? That's right!!!! Mr. Gorgeous Eyes. He was in line right behind me! An angel choir burst into a heavenly chorus of Hallelujah and cherubs danced joyfully on sunbeams while Handel conducted with a smile on his face. Or something like that. It was One of Those Moments. Where everything seems to come together and it all makes sense and it's amazing.

Little did I know...fuck. Why do I keep letting you know that I'm a complete stupid head? Ignore that foreshadowing, please. Please?

Thanks. It just slipped out. I didn't really mean it. Honestly. I am completely and totally an open book. That one was just a...a...Freudian slip. Not to be confused with one of those lace nightgowns that look so slippery, made of something like...satin? Yeah, I think that's the fabric. Or is it silk? Hmm...I'll have to check the next time I'm in a JCPenney. No judging; they have an excellent selection of nightwear. For real!

This is where the story gets really good, like in all of those Romantic Comedies you see on TV or in the theater; Mr. Gorgeous eyes swooped in, bought my coffee, sat with me at my favorite table (or my new favorite table because that's where we had our first coffee date) and had the best conversation with me about life, the universe and everything.

Of course, I knew that his name is Tyler and that he runs his own business and has a bazillion things going for him and is just the right age (3 years older than me).

My heart was beating rapidly, I had the shivers all up and down my body and I was sweating like a supermodel on a Manhattan runway. All the signs of a crush-made-real. And definitely a sign that I needed to buy new deodorant. Phew. Good thing we were just having coffee and there was no way on earth we would end up doing anything physical. Also, coffee breath. Eww. I decided that I should surreptitiously stop drinking the coffee and get a peppermint tea, instead. And one of those boxes of mints they have on sale by the registers. And a chocolate bar, to take the edge off. And then more mints to get rid of the chocolate—I would do all of this in the restroom; perfect plan!

"Oh, excuse me, Tyler, I'm just going to use the restroom."

I smiled beatifically and could totally feel him watching me (again) as I walked to the bathroom. In other words, he's into me. Thank God. Praise the Lord. And all that jazz. Crap. I had ended up in the bathroom with no mints. Or chocolate. What to do? Rinse? Did I have any toothpaste? Amazing. I love this purse; it holds absolutely everything I need.

I got it last April; it was 55% off at (you guessed it) JCPenney. It's a total Mary Poppins bag; holds everything but the kitchen sink. Well, actually, if you could split the sink in half and fold it twice, it would just about fit. It's a great bag. Has all kinds of pockets, too. A must have bag. I should tell all of my friends and then ask JCPenney for a commission on each bag I've sold through referrals.

I checked my hair, spit out the toothpaste and freshened up before realizing that before I left the bathroom, I should actually pee.

I took seven long hurried strides out of the bathroom and told Tyler that it had been really great but that I actually had to run (I didn't) because I was super busy (I wasn't) and that we'd have to get together again sometime to continue our discussion (yes, please!). I waited.

"Oh, sure. Not a problem. What's your number?" Yes! He asked me for mine; now it's not awkward at all that I asked for his, too.

I really had to tell George about this; I knew that he would just die. He had been telling me to find a boyfriend so that he didn't have to listen to all of my crap. *Oh, George. Just you wait. You're going to be so surprised. Soon my dear boy. Soon.*

That night, I picked up my phone and hit speed dial 7. The nighttime air beckoned to me out of the window and the moon was a pale version of half of a cheese wheel.

"George!"

"Nat, please. It's 1:00am."

His voice was all garbled with sleep, as if he'd swallowed a pillow, spat it back out, and had commenced talking with feathers stuck to his gums...

"I know! But I'm way too psyched to sleep! Remember Mr. Gorgeous Eyes?"

"Who?"

Now he sounded kind of pissed. Oops. Maybe he had stubbed his toe? Or swallowed one of the feathers and it went down the wrong pipe?

Maybe his plumbing was on the fritz! Or—maybe he just didn't care and wanted to go back to sleep. Nah.

"The guy in Starbucks, the super hunky one."

"Who?"

Definitely swallowed a feather. And now he was deaf!

"Mr. Gorgeous Eyes! Well, whatever, he asked me out! Well, not really, but he will, I just know it. He asked for my number and everything. He bought me coffee! We talked and talked and talked. It was amazing!"

Silence on the other end. Then, a yawn.

"Okay okay. Why do I need to know this now? I'm going back to sleep. Tell me about this wonder man later. Bye."

Wonder man? He hung up.

Hmmph.

George can be so rude, sometimes. Honestly.

Okay, so I know that stories are supposed to make sense and follow a linear path and all of that, but I'm going to break the rules. Big time. And, hey, it's my story so why not? Because, now, I see it clearly. Like one of those mountains that's shrouded in fog and then suddenly it's out there for everyone to see it. The fog sucked back to where it came from, God's maid finally hoovering the bit of earth she forgot last week.

Tyler is not a good guy. In fact, Tyler did not bump into me accidentally. He did not see me for the first time when he looked up from his phone in Starbucks, when I first saw him. He did not guess that I'd love to meet a guy in a coffee shop and see him wearing a nice suit, clean shaven and dressed to impress.

Tyler e-stalked me. Big time. I'm going to drop the proverbial other shoe...Tyler is Mr. Anon guy from Ask A Friend.

Dun dun dun.

I know. Totally freaky. Whacked. He researched me

and commented on all of my answers and then found out my favorite Starbucks and showed up and then used his insider knowledge to chat me up, get my phone number, gain my trust...

You know, in all of those Romantic Comedies, when the guy goes to all those lengths to get the girl...you never actually stop and think about the creep factor. Holy Shit. CREEPY! Don't you think? Okay, now, some would argue, all of that stuff is put on the internet by you and you let those people see everything...but but but it's still creepy. Right? Yes.

And, also flattering.

Because, Tyler did go to all the trouble of reading all of my answers and going through each line and then remembering important details and wearing clothes I liked and doing things to impress me. But, he also wasn't being himself. He was acting. He was pretending to be what I most wanted because I gave him the blueprint. It was all there. In all of my answers, he could see exactly what I wanted.

And he could pretend to give it to me.

Of course—who really knows what they want? And, once they get it, who really actually thinks it's all that great, anyway?

Poor Tyler. He didn't stand a chance. He was banking on my answers actually being in tune with what I really wanted, deep down. Not just what I said I wanted. Or wrote. Or answered. Or thought. See? Tricky, tricky, tricky. Only, I wasn't just tricking Tyler. I tricked myself, too. Because...he was the dream guy who did all of the things I said I wanted!

Faced with that—what's a girl to do but think she's falling madly in love?

George heard about all of the things Tyler was doing for me; I told him about the flowers Tyler sent to my desk (Chrysanthemums, not roses, because I had specifically said that somewhere in my answers, though I had forgotten and was totally bowled over that he had picked the flowers that I loved loved loved, as if by magic!).

George told me that flowers die fast and are a waste of money. Just like Cher from "Moonstruck", or, technically, Loretta Castorini. Maybe George is a Nicolas Cage fan.

I've never asked him.

It's such a shame; I thought I was so suave, capturing Tyler's interest in a Starbucks; meeting a stranger across a crowded room and all that. It's the kind of stuff that dreams are made of and he made it come true for me. I was the star of my very own Romantic Comedy. And, just so that I wouldn't get too comfortable, Tyler continued his shenanigans as Anon guy on Ask A Friend.

Even while we were dating! Even after I showed him the comments (two weeks into our fledgling relationship, still growing fuzz and waiting for the wings to come in so we could fly) and told him Anon guy had been plaguing my page and my answers for over a year (yes, a year! Psycho Stalker Tyler!)

He didn't have any tells (that I could see, anyway, but, again, I was wearing Rosy colored glasses). He just smiled at me and said not to worry about the comments (like George had said numerous times before) and that my answers were perfect and look at all of the points I had?

Smarmy, changing the topic of conversation bastard!

Tyler lulled me into a complete state of bliss; I thought we had the perfect relationship. He said all the right things at all the right times (bought me more

Chrysanthemums and wrote "I love you" for the first time in a card nestled within their blooms) (melt). I know. I know what you're thinking. How the hell could he know that I wanted that? No, I didn't write it down in an answer on Ask A Friend. But, I had written a post about it once on Facebook; that it would be great to get flowers and read an "I love you" first before it was spoken aloud because it would be different and oh so romantic...Tyler must really have an obsession.

Oh, yeah, and before I forget, Tyler also made me an origami crane (or so he pretended...he had one of his friends do it, I'm sure) and made it so that it could fly and had it sent to my office so I could display it proudly on my desk and make all of the other CPAs wild with envy at my crafty and considerate boyfriend. I had actually said something like that in an answer once, but, how was I supposed to remember I'd said that? Or hinted at it? Really, Tyler knew more about my answers than I did. And I wrote them!

When I told George about the crane, he spit out his ginger ale.

"He did what?" Ginger ale spewed forth indiscriminately and splattered all over my nice button down shirt. Yuck.

"George! You got me all wet!"

He started coughing; ginger ale is kind of spicy, isn't it? Even if you're not spitting it out from surprise, it can make you cough if you're not careful.

"I don't think Tyler is a man." George was still coughing.

"You're just jealous."

Who's a man, anyway? And what does it mean to be a man? It's certainly not what's sung in that Disney song—"mysterious as the dark side of the moon..."? Are you kidding? Men are open books.

"It's not possible that he's doing all of this. And you like this?" George looked aghast. I had no perspective, though; it was all, "oh so romantic."

"Yes! He's really in tune with his feminine side." I hit George on the shoulder. "He's really sensitive and sweet and he appreciates me and..."

"Is he gay?"

ARGH! What a stereotypical and down right prejudiced thing to say!!!

"NO! And I can't believe you just said that! So sexist!" I mean, God! I hit him again on the shoulder, much harder. Closed fist. Squeezed tight.

"Calm down. It's just a simple question. About his sexual orientation. Which is important, since you're straight. You need to make sure he is, too."

George's voice was calm and matter of fact. He rubbed his arm a bit. Oops; must have hit him a bit too hard.

Leave it to George to try to make it sound academic.

"Well, he's not. Once you meet him, you'll know."

I still hadn't gotten them to meet each other then; George was always mysteriously busy on the days Tyler could meet. "Why haven't you met him yet? He's my boyfriend and you're my best friend. You have to meet him."

"Yeah, I will. Chill." He rubbed his arm some more.

"I'm sorry. I didn't mean to hit you so hard. Do you need ice?"

"It's okay. I'm fine. Thanks." He took another sip of ginger ale and I felt guilty. I told myself in my head that I'd make it up to him.

"So, any progress on Mr. Anon guy? Have you found him yet?" I was so curious about his identity; I had to know. But, I also was feeling protective of Tyler and kind of wanted to change the subject. He's so NOT gay. Not even close.

"Nope. Not yet. I'll tell you when I find something, okay?" He burped twice and coughed again.

"Yeah, sure." I tried not to sound too disappointed; when would I find out?

Well, we know now it was Tyler. Sneaky git. That's some British slang; I like it. Wanker. Git. Knobhead.

Where was I?

Oh, yeah. Tyler booked a trip for us, a mini vacation, and I was so excited because I'd always wanted to go to Disney World and I'd never ever gone and he bought tickets and surprised me with the whole thing. You guessed it (though it really shouldn't be a surprise by now), I'd written an answer about it and he had read it. I had forgotten, again, about that answer. Really, when you write a lot of answers, it's easy to forget. Especially when your answers can span two or three years. You try it. See how many you remember.

And, it was on the trip that George finally found something out. A big something. But, it wasn't because of his computer hacking skills. Or, not really, anyway.

I asked him to feed my cat while we were gone and to collect my mail and water my plants. George is a really really good friend; but, I was also paying him a bit of money to do this. It's only fair. He didn't know about the money, of course, until I got back. I had put the cash in an envelope and pushed it under his door. 100% anonymously. But I wonder...

George was so excited about the free money he told me about it the next day. Ha!

Tyler left his laptop at my place because in the rush to leave we had forgotten it among the jumble of bags and things that I was desperate to bring with us. Tyler had to persuade me to leave my pink over-the-shoulder Vera Bradley bag behind and we found out later I'd stuffed his laptop in it. Oops. That was a major tiff in the airport; to go back and get it or stay?

I told him he could use mine and he forgave me. I think. I mean, do you ever really know if people forgive you? They could just be lying to you. And pretending that they did. But, meanwhile, under cover of darkness, they really didn't forgive you and are waiting to pounce when your back is turned so that you scream and reveal your location to the waiting jungle cat.

George found out it was Tyler. That he was Mr. Anon guy. It was all there on his laptop. There was a folder marked "NSA" and, naturally, George opened it. I mean, how was he to know it stood for Natalie Silver's Answers? You see a folder marked "NSA" on the laptop of your best friend's significant other and you OPEN that file. Obviously.

That's a no-brainer.

Though, now that I think of it, George had to open the laptop, turn it on and boot it up to find that file...but, you know, either way. You find a file like that, you open it. And copy it. And send it to yourself to read later.

Of course. And then get rid of all traces of your meddling on the computer. At least, I think you can do that. George probably knows how.

George didn't know what to do next. After uncovering that nasty little secret. Mr. Anon guy...not so Anon, after all. Well, he did know, obviously, that he had to tell me. But he didn't know how he was going to break it to me. Especially since, to all outward observers, I was head-over-heels for Tyler.

Who's to say how I would have reacted to the news?

I don't even know. I couldn't tell you how I would've reacted. But, after the Disney World trip, after spending significant amounts of time with Tyler one on one, I was starting to fall out of my dream world. There's only so much you can take of the most romantic stuff ever. Poems left on your pillow, spa packages waiting at the hotel, candlelit dinners...after awhile, you start to wonder: what are all of these perks hiding? Why so many bells and whistles? Is there a jalopy underneath this shiny bodywork?

It hit me the day we were on our way back: we hadn't really once had a really deep conversation the whole trip. Anytime I tried to bring up something like our emotions, beyond "I love you" or where we might be headed or what exactly he wanted out of life, he would change the subject or subtly shift the conversation so I was answering my own questions and he was "hmming" and nodding.

Also, anytime we shifted beyond the material covered in my answers (not that I knew that's what was happening, at the time) he would make a noncommittal answer and never give me his true opinion. Of course, he couldn't give me his true opinion. He wanted me to tell him what I wanted him to say. Or write about it. Then he could sweep me off my feet by saying the exact thing I wanted.

It was a kind of drug for him, I think. Seeing that look of wonder on my face and delight that he had hit the nail on the head with whatever he had said. He never wanted me to be confused by what he said or dislike it or challenge it. He just wanted me to lap it up like it was cream and he was giving it to me for free and it had no calories but tasted exactly like cream...

I hadn't really put this into words, though. My discomfiture. My growing realization that I didn't think I really knew much about Tyler at all. And we had been dating for six months!

As these things go, George had me over for dinner at his house (which was really just Chinese take out because he can't cook at all) and I started to tell him that I was feeling a bit disillusioned. George had finally met Tyler, before our trip to Disney World, but the two hadn't hit it off well. They both told me separately that they'd prefer to spend as little time with each other as possible. I told George that our relationship was six months old and I didn't know anything too deep about Tyler. I also drank a bit more wine than usual. Chinese food is salty.

"Nat, what are you saying? I thought this guy was Mr. Perfect and said all the right things and knew you so well it was scary." George was wearing the black and white sweater I've always liked on him and he had gotten a haircut. Huh. He reminded me of someone, but I couldn't put my finger on who.

Maybe...Atticus Finch? Gregory Peck? It slipped my mind. Maddening.

"I know, he does seem perfect. But, I'm starting to think he's either too perfect or I don't actually like the Mr. Perfect I thought I did. Does that make sense?"

I looked over at him and slurped some more wine. I'm not a picky wine drinker; as long as it's drinkable, I'm fine. But that one tasted really good. Maybe I should become more of a wine snob; I could get a Wine Club membership or something.

"NSA..." George mumbled.

"What was that?" I thought I had heard him say, "NSA."

"Nat, I found something. On Tyler's computer." He

looked worried.

"He's in the NSA??? What?? Oh my God! Maybe this explains everything! How he knows so much about me...has he been spying? Has the country been spying on me??" I was, to tell the truth, a bit drunk. The country couldn't possibly want to spy on me. I'm so average.

"Nat, calm down! No, he's not in the NSA. But...the reason he knows so much about you is because he *has* been spying on you." I must have looked horrified because he said, "Not the country! But, just him. Look."

And I saw it all; the whole file. It made me sick. Or maybe that was the wine...I really had had too much.

"George, oh my God." I clicked through and saw all my answers. And his notes about my answers. All of his snide comments, all of his punctuation marks, things the moderators would never have let him post on the actual site.

I sat down. Well, actually, fell on the floor. George knelt down beside me and rubbed my back and all of a sudden I was crying and sobbing and sniveling all over his nice sweater. Sorry, George.

"I ccaan't be-believe th—this." I stuttered. Or maybe slurred. The wine was quite potent, after all. But, I was crying loudly. With increasing despair. For seven straight minutes. Maybe eleven.

Deceit and betrayal gave me their bitter fruit. Much worse than salty pork dumplings.

I felt Tyler's knife throbbing through my beautiful, 55% off, JCPenny pink top; this was like learning that the folks who raised you weren't really your parents but were actually alien robots designed to look and act like your parents. In the meantime, your real parents were residing on Pluto and had no memory of you at all.

Erased?

It was also quite illuminating; now I knew how Tyler had known so much about me. Sweet Tyler (can you feel my sarcasm) knew exactly how to do and say the things that would get my heartstrings singing. And now I knew why he was so in touch with his feminine side. I had, of course, wondered about that, too. But you never like to really admit that, especially to yourself, that maybe your boyfriend is actually gay...

I don't know how long I cried but eventually I said, "What do I do now?"

"Break up with him. Or..."

"Or what? Of course I have to break up with him! This is sick! He's obsessed with me!" (I've always wanted to say something like that.)

"Well, you know that he's Anon guy. Now you could mess with his head." *George...I never knew you were so devious. Or did I? I can't remember.*

"How? I'd have to act! He'd see right through me." I finally blew my nose and felt somewhat normal again.

"You don't have to do it forever; just a few days. Maybe a week. Then break up with him." George is brilliant.

He came up with the whole plan; all I had to do was act on it. I think George had been thinking about this the whole time we'd been at Disney World. It was too brilliant to be a spur-of-the-moment thing.

Here's what we planned: I would pretend like I hadn't found out and I would write ten answers to questions and say the opposite of what I actually thought. Then, when Tyler trotted forth what he thought I wanted, I'd look all confused and sulky and say, "That's not what I want!"

Awesome.

Of course, he didn't fall for it. And, it was getting really hard for me to let him kiss me or to suggest dinners or walks and the week was almost up. I had ten answers all lined up for him to fall for and he hadn't. I was getting desperate. I really wanted to see his face when I told him that he had gotten it all wrong.

Finally, I called in reinforcements. "George, how do we trip him up? He hasn't said one thing about my recent answers."

"Has he posted comments?" George sounded like he was in the supermarket. Typical. Always buying snacks and junk food.

"Yes, of course. Anon guy never misses an answer." It was so dumb, now that I knew it was Tyler; he commented on my answers but I couldn't get him to fall into the trap I'd set.

"OK, well, comment back. Try to get him to reveal something online and then in real life, too. Call him at the same time you see an Anon comment pending." George really is devious.

"What if he doesn't fall for it?" I bit my nails. It was starting to make my cuticles suffer! Not that I really did much with my cuticles, anyway.

"Then, just break up with him and tell him you know about the Anon thing." George sounded too cheerful...then again, he wasn't dating a psycho.

"Okay." I hung up and hugged myself. How to do this?

I got online and started commenting like crazy on all of his comments. *You should start your critiques like this; how come you don't comment on what you liked? Why are you so obsessed with my answers.* Cough cough.

Finally, I called him on the phone, just as I saw another Anon comment pending.

"Tyler! Hi, are you busy?" Phone conversations are so easy...you can totally fake things on the phone. My face gives away all of my thoughts, so phone calls were my mainstay with Tyler that week.

Anonymous comment...still pending.

"Kind of; I'm working." He was distracted, naturally.

"Working? At this hour?" It was 10:00pm at night; I knew for a fact that he always got done at 8:30pm on the dot. He never worked past then. Never.

"Oh, right. Not really working, um, but thinking about work." I had him. Hopefully. Crossed fingers.

"What are you thinking about?" **Anon comment...posted**.

Anonymous: *I'm not obsessed with your answers.*

"Are you obsessed with my answers?" Crossed fingers and toes; my voice was bubbly and light and frothy and totally unsuspicious.

"No, not at all. I'm giving you constructive criticism to make them better." GOTCHA!

"You are? Really?" Muah ha ha ha ha.

"What?" He sounded panicked.

"You're the Anon; don't try to hide it. I know you are." My voice was hard. Exactly as I had practiced it that morning. While pretending to train a gun at the bad guy.

"I don't know what you're talking about." He was really backing himself into a corner.

"Yes, you do. You're the Anon on Ask A Friend. I just saw your comment. But, also, I've seen the file. NSA. On your computer." There. Let him think about that.

"I've never let you see..." Major Gotcha!

"Never let me see your laptop? Maybe not, but now

I know for sure. You just gave yourself away. I can't believe you would do this; spy on me and stalk me and all. We're breaking up, right now. I don't want to hear from you again. And if you comment on any of my answers again, I'll tell the moderators and get you banned permanently from the site."

And that, as they say, was that. Well, not quite. He tried to get me back, sent flowers, etc., but who was he kidding? As soon as I found out about his underhandedness, there was no way I could trust him again. Plus, some of those comments were really quite hurtful (the ones that the moderators didn't see, of course). They were just some answers on a website; no need to get so personal about it. Or so mean.

George called and I'm going to go catch a movie with him later; I started to put on jeans and a t-shirt but decided to wear this really nice red dress I got and forgot to take to Disney World. I was going to wear it to dinner on that trip, but, what the hell. I may as well wear it now. I think George likes the color red; I think I heard him say that once.

I wonder what the movie is about...maybe it's another Romantic Comedy where the girl falls for her best friend in the end...

Nah. That would be too cliché.

Love Eats Dark Chocolates

Last Saturday night, I was already on the roof of my penthouse in the Empire State Building when she announced the pink box.

First there was her voice—cheerful on top but slightly menacing—ha ha—shouting, almost singing. Then came that unique laughter I had known and loved for many years. The words flowing out like endless rain through her demon mouth and the vaguely European accent. Then, his voice came, tenor to her soprano, high and gay as always.

Downstairs, little feet would soon awaken from their golden slumbers and join. Love was in the air. The dusk bit the last of the blue as the evening sky over Manhattan faded to black. A nice July evening in 2040. Things were much different in 2014, when I was much younger.

By the time the 4th of July rolled in back then, I was at the end of my rope. Even though California held the promise of an endless summer, the solstice was over. My logical brain knew that the days were getting shorter. And darker. I was totally burnt out, like a toast left too long in the microwave. Not that I have heard of too many people who microwave toast; they typically go to the International Pancake Mansion. IPM for short. But this begs the question: what in God's green earth is so international about IPM? Some mysterious questions in life are best left unanswered.

I was at the end of my rope because I had gone through many bad relationships with women. Yes, sir and madam, you see, I didn't have any of the common Californian addictions that other people had. Getting your doctor to write you a prescription so you could buy marijuana at the local supermarket, or pretending to be a wine connoisseur so you could polish away 4.4 glasses every day in a socially acceptable way without people thinking that you were an alcoholic—probably, mostly because they were too drunk and self-absorbed to notice anything but themselves. Just sayin'. Ha ha!

Such was life in the summer of 2014, in Redondo Beach California. Back then, before the secession happened, Redondo Beach was actually part of the sprawling Los Angeles megapolis.

I was very fond of the Redondo Beach Boardwalk and all of the pretty girls strolling in their summer clothes. Even though every day I lived I got older—this probably happens to everyone—I looked much younger than my biological age. And on a good day, even more so. Blame it on my good Asian genes, two scoops of coconut oil, and of course chocolate. Lots and lots of chocolates.

But those women. Ahh, yes, the women. They were as perplexing as one of those Internet games I would play twenty three hours a day. And as flaky as a bowl of cornflakes drenched in milk and honey.

There was the Norwegian blonde, Ingrid Christismyonlyson. Or something like that. I don't know. Her curly hair partially covered her turquoise blue eyes as she swayed the hips on her 187.96 centimeter (6 feet 2 inches) body, oh so slowly. That drove the men crazy. Crazy enough they just opened up their wallets and bought her drinks, dinner, and mozzarella cheese sticks all night long. All hoping for a cuddle or a kiss. Often promised, rarely delivered.

"I love mozzarella cheese sticks, they are so American." Ingrid smiled angelically. She was wearing clothes that made her look like a model who shopped at Walmart. Since I am Asian and cheap, I liked that.

"Ingrid, um, mozzarella cheese sticks are Italian," I said.

"Whatever, ha ha." Ingrid rolled her eyes. She looked so cute at that moment. She interlocked her fingers with mine and tugged me toward the bar.

I first met Ingrid in a strip club two days before, when we were arguing about who would get the next lap dance from a dark haired entertainer named Oprah. Turns out the stripper had a big heart. And ended up giving both of us a lap dance together, for only 50% more than we could have gotten for separate lap dances. What a deal. It was some song from one of those one-hit wonder girl bands. From Norway, or Denmark, or Sweden, who knows? Like ABBA. From one of those Scandinavian countries. Outside of my Asian homeland and California, my geographic knowledge is quite limited.

The first night we met, Ingrid told me that, in Norway, the sequence of dating is quite different than it is in America. You meet someone and on the same night, you hook-up. Sleep with them.

"THEN! and only THEN," Ingrid giggled as she

tossed her hair like an avocado salad, "you decide whether to date. Or not." She finished. "If you are okay after you have been intimate, then you start dating." Ingrid licked the pink lipstick on her lips. Slowly. My eyes were locked on her and she smelled like cotton candy mixed with roses.

"But, Ingrid, aren't there different kinds of intimacy?" I asked. And then answered my own question, "Physical, sexual, intellectual, emotional?"

Ingrid giggled. "You are so cute. Look around this bar! Come on! Do you think any guy wants to discuss philosophy with me?" Ingrid flirted.

She started running her fingers through my dark Asian hair like a cat kneading her owner. I swore I could hear soft purring. Not sure if it was me or Ingrid. The dusty jukebox at the corner started playing a romantic song from the 1950's as two guys in cowboy hats started dancing with each other.

I gazed deeply into Ingrid's eyes, except, I am not sure...it may have been into the great light beer in the glass mug that she was drinking and I was siphoning off little by little. The 1950's song ended, the dancing cowboys had shifted to the cheap motel next to the dive bar, and John Lennon was singing about love. I looked at Ingrid and focused my gaze; she was still gently brushing my hair. Her left hand found my knees. Caress, said her left hand to my melting knees. It was only my knee, but I imagined that caress elsewhere. Zing! Ingrid infatuation. This had nothing to do with love from my perspective. Love is a choice. This was LUST. Plain and simple. Tons of chemicals blended with chocolate and alcohol.

According to the Norwegian code, that was the night I would taste the pleasures of Ingrid. Ahh...momentarily, my logical brain had forgotten that

John Lennon said that life is what happens when you are busy making other plans.

At 2:00 AM, when Ingrid and I were tightly hugging each other, lips dancing the tango, the bearded philosopher guy approached.

Ingrid was rubbing her pretty painted fingers on my shoulders when he said hello. Right at that moment, I had a premonition. An inkling that things weren't going to end the way I expected. Funny thing about life: it never ends the way you want it to. Ha ha. Soon, I would be laughing on the outside, crying on the inside.

The bearded dude kept blabbing on about philosophy and every philosophical construct he talked about had woman's pleasure as the centerpiece. He kept pulling out books from his $9,800 leather bag. No imitation Chinatown stuff there...that was the real deal. The books had crimson red covers and dust coated them like crushed candy and nuts over a hot fudge, chocolate ice cream sundae. And don't forget lots and lots of chocolate.

Very suspicious. But I could see by Ingrid's eyes and her feet angled toward him that it was working. Always watch the feet. Feet don't lie. They say that there are two tongues in every person and the tongue in the foot never lies.

"I am ready to go home. For Action. But I..." Ingrid started. She was clearly mid-sentence but I interrupted her. Better to cut the bearded dude off at the knees and grab this opportunity. Carpe Diem!

"I will get the bar tab," I said. I was already sprinting toward the bar, hey ho, let's go to the land of amazing Norwegian love. I didn't know how I had pulled it off, going home with Ingrid, but I seemed to have.

After I paid the $88 bar tab—ten glasses of alcohol for Ingrid, one for me, and a 19.2% tip—I rushed back to Ingrid's side where I could see the bearded guys' hands on her hips, moving them up and down like a guy about to shoot a basketball. Ingrid was tugging his beard as Kenny Rogers played some country song on the jukebox. A sad song. The dude's beard looked like Abraham Lincoln's or Sigmund Freud's; I forget, did Freud even have a beard? For one moment, I was convinced that it was actually Kenny Rogers slowly seducing the seductress Ingrid away from me.

Ingrid's eyes were sparkling like the *Twinkle, Twinkle, Little Star* nursery rhyme every good Asian boy learns in his early schooling in Asia. But I wasn't a good Asian boy when I lived there. Ergo, I only remembered the title. Her feet were pointed towards the door. I guess we should stick with the sayings— they will never lead us astray. Ingrid voted with her feet. She called out my name.

"Sorry! I am not going home with you tonight." She tugged the dude's beard.

"And—what's up with your name, anyway?" Ingrid giggled. "That's not a real Asian name! Do you even like your name?" Ingrid asked.

"I do. I love my name," I said (even though I don't).

My parents picked my name from a character on a syndicated American cable show that only foreign audiences could love.

"Ingrid, what happened to us going home together and hooking-up tonight?" I asked, hoping for one more chance.

"I guess I lied—we all do that." Ingrid dashed out of the dive bar door into a black limousine.

Either the bearded guy was a trust fund baby or,

more than likely these days, he had a $25 coupon off Uber. I don't know. But I know that romance had cheated me.

I went to a 24-hour-diner hoping to write really poignant, meaningful and concise poetry. I ended up having a bunch of bacon and toast and went home. No poetry.

As I sprawled out on my couch and turned on some late night show on HBO, I reminded myself that the greatest love of all was self-love. I practiced a lot of self-love that night.

After Ingrid, there was the beautiful brunette, Bulgarian-Italian. She referred to herself in the third person a lot. Like every third word. She said, at twenty-two, she was an old-soul and that we should have an eternal relationship that transcends all time. Kinda like that movie with the time traveler and his wife, except more romantic.

Yes, I am a traditional Asian dude and a sucker for sappy sweet romance and creamy chocolates. My romantic feelings toward Bulgarian-Italian chick were not so much when she asked me for $250,000 for her sex-change surgery. In return, she promised me, she would be mine until she changed her...mind.

Her favorite saying went like this, "I am a woman. What do I want? I don't know. When do I want it? Now."

I kissed her and she tasted like fine Belgian chocolate. That was the day before her surgery—minus my money.

Then came Pretty Penny. A redhead who was the Playboy bunny of the month. When she invited me to dinner and answered the door in a chocolate gown, I heard some sweet Asian melody in my head. My infatuation buzz lasted until we got up to the kitchen and her husband was there.

"Don't you like an open-marriage? You are a technology guy and Asian, open-minded and smart!" Penny pouted like that character on *24*, the Queen of Pout, Chloe, and then pointed to the bedroom upstairs.

If Chloe ever pointed like that to Jack, he would have given her one of those death stares of his and then the ominous, counting clock would have appeared, leaving viewers wondering what exactly Jack was doing to Chloe during the commercial break.

I enjoyed eating at McDonald's that night.

All the while, I took comfort in the stability of my relationship with a sweet, 23-year-old Australian named Coral. She had long, wavy blonde hair, eyes blue as the ocean and she looked eighteen. She was significantly younger than me, but, mind you, as long as people are over eighteen and it's consensual, all is fair in love. And, as I would soon find out, war.

"It's a stripper's name," Coral flirted.

We had just met at a hackathon, a computer coding event. Where 99% of the attendees are men who make software as they drink gallons of soda and tuck away dozens of pizzas. Given that Coral is hot, every guy was hitting on her. Everyone except me. I went up to her on the pretense of wanting to be her friend and to protect her from the creepy technology dudes.

Don't get me wrong—I did want to help her. But I pretty much wanted to make love to her, too. Like every other guy at the event. I was wearing a mask. But isn't romantic love all about wearing a mask?

Over the course of six months, we slept together hundreds of times. Man oh man, it was good. We had an open relationship. I was always insecure about it, because, objectively, she is a hot woman. Hot. Very Hot. Insecurity walked in and built a village.

Soon, though, I would meet a man who would change that. A man—not a woman.

Coral wrote me a letter. It could be called one of the first Exhibits leading up to a Skirmish that would eventually turn into a War.

She wrote:

A list of things you asked me to write down for you

1) Why we're special:

-   The   amazing   and   unique,   incomparable, connection that we have

- The family relationship we share

- The business interests we are pursuing as a team

- The fact we never wear masks around each other

- The fact you are privy to every element of my life and vice versa

- The fact I will let you, and in fact encourage, you getting to know and communicate with Jerry, have had you talk to Jasmine, and will eventually do the same with Eric (eg, people who matter to me all being involved with each other on some level)

- The fact you have keys to my home (this may seem small but given my security concerns due to Marcel etc, it's a big thing).

- The fact I let you keep food in my fridge, a toothbrush in my bathroom and clothes in a drawer which is just YOUR drawer

- This is a very big thing after Marcel, VERY big to me

- I have let you see me eat KFC multiple times (again, a BIG thing to me. I'd probably even let you see me eat a T-bone. These are things I do not let just anyone do)

- There   is   more   besides   that   relating   to   the

different ways in which we help each other etc.

- If you want to get sexual about it, which we shouldn't be doing because it makes it seem like it should matter, which it doesn't—

- You don't have to wear a condom

- Your mouth is allowed near my ass (I'm not comfortable letting anyone else do this)

- We have our Daddy/Daughter thing (although to me this is not primarily sexual)

2) Why you are putting too much weight on the sex thing:

- You immediately jump to me having sex with someone else as them somehow being a threat to our relationship and your position in my life, disregarding ALL of the above—you get crazy and define us only by sex when you do that. "We have sex, now she's having sex with someone else for a few days, my spot isn't safe" etc.

- If I had a friend who I loved come here for a week, and I didn't see you because I was busy with them and hadn't seem them in a long time, or whatever—you wouldn't be threatened at all

- You weren't threatened by Cooper and I love him a LOT and just spent almost a week seeing him pretty much daily. I was far more "intimate" with him than the guy I fucked or anyone I'm likely to fuck in the future, minus Eric, of course.

- It is only when sex is added that you blindly ignore all other elements

- That is what you need to work on here, taking a step back and realizing not everything is about sex—in fact almost nothing is about sex

- The other thing you need to work on is the insecurity; and that WILL pass given time and a few

situations like this where you realize you have no control, nor should you, but that it is nothing bad and you don't need to have control to ensure your spot is safe and that I am not going anywhere

- You can get insecure and we can work on it but you can't let it make you possessive—and trying to have a say over what I do with my body, short of protection, which impacts us both, is not a healthy attitude

- (For example, when you are having sex and fooling around with others, me getting controlling and trying to say you couldn't go near another girl's ass would be a problem for you, I hope—and if not, it SHOULD be and we can discuss that too. Your sexuality belongs to you and unless you are harming another person or putting them at risk, no one should ever have any say over what you do with your own body for any reason, sexual or not)

- Now, everything is fine—review why we are special, realize there is no threat to you or your position, you aren't being replaced, nothing is changing, there is no reason to feel threatened, nothing bad is going to happen as a result of this

3) Yes, you have things you need to work on, and I'll help you with those all I can and we will get there —but everything is OK. Max will come, I'll be busy anyway as I would have been regardless, I'll still manage to see you, you'll see there's no threat, it will pass quickly and you'll be a little more secure as a result—but in the meantime, review why we are special without only focusing on the sexual parts that are unique to us, because sex does not define who we are and although I do enjoy having sex with you, the only reason it is important to me is because we are working on helping your mental health and happiness there—yes we'd still have sex otherwise and enjoy it and all of that—but would it be IMPORTANT to me? No.

4) What we have has very, very little to do with sex

- I hope this helps. Love you lots. xx

- *In addition, I actually use the bathroom around you and let you use my bathroom. XD

I loved her deeply. Even when she told me that our open relationship was now closed to me because the ex-Navy seal she met at a conference in Barcelona was writing her a check for thirty thousand dollars for five months' expenses. I used to give her five thousand dollars every month.

I guess some people would call her a prostitute. That's one surefire way to shatter your romantic illusions—realize your girl is a prostitute.

I was delusional and I moved on. Coral lied. Our entire relationship was a lie. But, then again, since life results in death...isn't life a lie?

Nonetheless, I never let go of my notion of eternal love. But I realized that there are many types of love. And my logical, software scientist brain told me that you can't get all the types of love from one person. At least, the probability is as low as you getting swallowed up by a Japanese space monster while eating 55% Cacao bittersweet chocolate in the park.

As August rolled around like a lion, I began to regain some of my hope, even though my bank account was considerably lower as a result of my dalliances. Or as they say back home, "Those girls sucked your money like a vampire mosquito sucks your blood." Trust me, it sounds seventy-seven percent funnier in my native Asian tongue. Ha ha!

One day, as dusk rolled around (like a monkey, instead of a lion, this time), I was standing on my block, gazing out at the Pacific Coast Highway. It accents the ocean like a chocolate layer on an ice cream cake.

As I gazed, I started to dance; I shook and gyrated my hips. Sometimes, I eat a gyro while gyrating. Twerking—as the kids call it. Word!

Some of the guys who lived on my street rode by on their thousand dollar Schwinns and asked if I were "gay". I rolled my eyes, batted my eyelashes, and twirled my hips—much like I did at my Saturday night Bachata (THE forbidden Latin dance) class and said, "YES! Heck YEAH!" Of course I was happy! Borderline giddy. I was playing games and pursuing my one true love—consuming copious, colorful chocolate.

Then, back to back, two events happened that changed my perspective. Totally unplanned. But a great man once said that, "Life, despite all our careful planning, is plotless." Or something like that. I don't know. Not quite as eloquent when you translate it from my native Asian tongue.

The first event took place at the local supermarket between the salami and the organic, vegan, faux beef jerky aisle. I was standing underneath a million-watt bright light that made it seem like we were already in heaven. She was gorgeous with blonde hair and eyes as green as Kermit the Frog.

But, she was much prettier than Ms. Piggy. She initiated the conversation, invited me to dinner at her house the next night, and asked me for my phone number. As she was texting me, the smile on my face was wider than the continent of Europe. An old Elvis Presley song came to me as I was looking at her soft, pink top. I was dreaming of cuddling in her lap and eating milk chocolate. I dreamed of writing her a poem about the stars, love, and chocolate. Not sure if chocolates would survive the first edit.

"OMG! This is so totally cool!" She spoke like a typical California girl. Totally!

"Like, I have plans with my girlfriend Taylor—" (every girl under 30 in 2014 California was named either Morgan or Taylor) "—but I will cancel." She giggled. "Whatev," she said, shaking her booty.

She scratched her nails on my shoulder. They were all Japanesey with designs and cute flowers and geometric shapes on them. I was beginning to really believe that those bright lights were like some UFO and they had lifted me out of the supermarket into heaven. Soon I would see Jesus and Buddha partying together and buying milk chocolate.

"I have a lot of gay friends and I am so excited that you and I can be gay BFFs. Awesome! I am feeling it!" She gushed.

"Gay BFF. Feeling it," I parroted, trying to sound cheerful. But shock and disappointment were surging through my body.

I forced a smile.

"Ha. Look—I am not gay." I dropped the bomb.

Her eyes enlarged to the point I was convinced—if only for a nanosecond—that they were flying saucers.

While I was debating whether or not I would complain to Jesus and Buddha about my bad luck with women, she did a one eighty and sprinted away from me faster than a running back with the ball on the 10 yard line, on 3rd and Goal.

I did text her the next day, asking if the dinner invitation was still good. "No guts, no glory," as I have learned from that Asian zen master karate god, Bruce Lee.

But, that incident got me thinking. What if—instead of being fully gay—I was a little gay? Would women trust me more? Would I be happy?

Who knows? Whatever will be will be. The future is not ours to see. Just live for your daily chocolate, one bar at a time.

After Coral and the other women left me, my large house felt empty. There were rubber duckies, edible massage lotions and half-used bottles of baby oil everywhere. The mess was bothering me so I went to one of those Internet cleaning sites, plunked down a hundred bucks and waited for the footsteps of my magical cleaner to appear at the door. I learned in an old Asian class that life is ephemeral. I think that the real ephemeral thing is a clean residence. And I hoped and prayed that my cleaner would give that to me.

From the moment Herbert walked in, took off his shoes, put down his cleaning supplies, and stood under the crown molding—next to my Salvatore Dali painting, you know the one with all the clocks shaped like chocolate colored pancakes—in my living room...I fell in love. A platonic love, not a sexual one. I could hear a chorus of Angels singing. Angels named Paul McCartney, Buddy Holly, Katy Perry, Miley Cyrus, and Adele. Especially Adele.

"Sir," Herbert's voice was melodic like an Irish folk ballad, "I will make sure your house is cleaner than my grandmother's beach house in Mexico."

"Ha ha, I knew it, you are Mexican?"

"No, born and raised in Redondo Beach," Herbert rejoined.

I felt stupid with my ethnic stereotyping.

"I am sorry Herbert. We are all Americans."

"It's OK, sir! Welcome here from Asia. I know Asia is a big country." Herbert nodded his head.

That proved to me that Herbert, with his bad grasp of basic geography, is a *true* American.

Herbert was the most meticulously methodical cleaner I have ever seen. Except my Asian grandmother—God rest her soul—when she cranked up Michael Jackson and almost glided like a dancer around the house, her vacuum like a laser beam extinguishing dust monsters. Or even a big Japanese monster like Godzilla.

Herbert's navy blue work pants were touching the marble bathroom floor as he almost rhythmically scrubbed away the mildew. In the background, Gloria Estefan sang about some dance they did on Miami Beach.

Herbert finished cleaning my house as the sunlight began to tiptoe away, yielding to a fast-dancing moonlight. I looked at Herbert and his full chocolate-colored eyes met mine. I felt warm. I looked at the stars peeking out from the side of the mountains and realized that the stars were there before me and they would be there after me. After all, we are all dust with eyes. Love is the only thing that survives. I hope I will find love again. I have faith that I will.

Then, suddenly, I realized that with Herbert I had love. Right there, in the moment. Albeit a different kind of love.

"Herbert, why don't you stay and have a cup of coffee?"

"Sir. It's against my company's rules. But—what the hell?" Herbert smiled.

He stayed for three cups of coffee and some chocolates. And he kept coming back every two weeks, like clockwork. 3.75 hours of cleaning followed by three cups of coffee. Usually another 60 minutes together. Other than my dog, Herbert became the only family I had. A gay cleaning person—ha ha! And we became close. I imagine that there are many, many different kinds of love.

After Herbert left, I figured, why not start going out with men? I could never see myself attracted to men sexually, but there is so much more to a relationship than sex. Intellectual bonding, shared interests, affections, emotional support...all while eating chocolates.

So I placed an ad on Craigslist. It read:

I am not gay. Not that there is anything wrong with being gay. I have many gay friends. And love them (in a non-sexual way). Looking for companionship, emotional support, and chocolates.

No long walks on the beach, that is like so clichéd.

I was excited when a guy named Gary answered the ad. Gary said he was a spiritual body builder and dated both men and women. I told him that we were not dating, it was strictly platonic, in Craigslist parlance. I went to meet him at the local café, Saturday afternoon at 3:03 PM. I make all of my appointments in palindrome time, since people are more apt to remember.

I was still on the sidewalk, closer to the door of an Italian restaurant nearby, when I noticed her sitting in the window, dipping her chocolate covered cookie into a smoldering cup of hot chocolate. She had long blonde hair that danced like a wave off of Redondo beach. Her eyes were green like a bottle of mineral water. At that moment, I thought they were green like a frog, but, you see, a frog isn't particularly romantic. And I wanted to feel romantic. After all, this was my first non-sexual date with a guy.

The girl had the face of an angel, her porcelain skin glowed. Her full lips were pink and she smiled impishly to reveal a set of perfect white teeth. Those veneers must have cost a fortune.

As I stood in line to order my organic latte, I noticed that she was writing and mumbling into her notebook...either that or laughing loudly. How inappropriate—does she laugh at funerals? But then I caught myself. Only God can judge you. Don't remember who said that. It was either a minister or Miley Cyrus.

I planted my butt in a chair at the table kitty-corner from her. I proceeded to take a damp napkin and started to wipe any dirt or food stains from the wooden surface of the table. Slowly. Methodically. Just like Herbert does.

What will Gary drink? Should I buy him a drink before he gets here? If we go up to get a drink, should I sit at the table and play it cool? Should I pay for it? Shh. Quiet, I told myself. This is not a date. Just a hangout with a friend. A new friend.

Maybe that's why all the women are gone. I like meeting new women. It may be my own fault. Gosh.

"Hi, you must be," a deep voice erupted next to my shoulder. I jumped up so hard that the girl kitty-corner from me started laughing. Gary could hear her, but his gaze was steady, focused on me.

"Hi, Gary! So nice to meet you," I squeaked.

He was a good looking guy; about 6'2 inches tall, with a lean muscular body, dark black hair, and large brown eyes. But, aside from his good looks, there was a certain presence and charisma about him.

"Please, sit down," I said in my normal voice.

Gary sat, took out a brown paper bag and put it down on the table.

"Hey, if you are Asian," (as if that were a question...) "what's up with your name?" Gary asked.

"Your name sounds like it's out of a John Wayne movie."

"Ha ha, yes, I am Asian, and my parents were watching a cable show when they conceived me. Probably."

Gary took a big, foot long missile out of the brown paper bag. Except it wasn't a missile; it was a meatball sandwich. He unwrapped the sandwich and began to speak.

"We are all empty inside. Biologically speaking of course," Gary posited.

I was staring at his meatball sandwich, dripping with red tomato sauce, punctuated by random shapes of stretched out melted mozzarella cheese. I am definitely empty inside now and would like to fill my insides with that meatball sandwich.

"So we try to fill the emptiness with money, pleasure and food," Gary continued. Then he took a big bite out of his meatball sandwich.

"You want some?" Gary belatedly looked up, mouth full. It came out as, "Ewe wahnd shome?"

"Yeah, whatev." I played it cool. Saliva pooled underneath my tongue.

My eyes kept finding the laughing girl because I felt like she was watching every move of the non-date Gary and I were enjoying courtesy of Craig, some 424 miles north in San Francisco.

Gary and I talked for over two hours and countless chocolates. We agreed to make a non-date at the same time next week. I was so excited.

After Gary left, I walked over to the girl. At first she was deeply engrossed in whatever she was writing and didn't notice me. Then she looked up and smiled.

"Look, you were watching me and my, um, friend," I stated, attempting to sound serious, but I could hardly suppress my laughter. I had the giggles. She seemed like the kind of girl that can give anyone the giggles.

She still hadn't said a word. I was seriously wondering if she could speak when she opened her mouth and, bam, I heard her accent.

"Hello, he he. How was your date with your gay friend?" She belly laughed.

"Gosh, I assumed you were an all American girl," I said, surprised.

"Don't assume. Tsk tsk tsk, you nice American boy. Don't you know what they say—it makes an ass out," she started—but couldn't finish because, at this point, her own laughter seemed to take over her body and her inexplicable joy was pouring out like endless rain into a flower vase on the patio.

"Yes, Gary is gay. And his voice is high. But he is just a friend. I am taking a break from women. And I am American but of Asian ethnicity." I kept wondering the whole time when she would come up for air. She must have strong lungs.

"So you are bisexual. Ha ha ha ha ha ha ha ha ha —" She was actually loling. I thought people only did that online. True laughing-out-loud behavior. Over nothing. Seriously, where does her joy come from??

"Asia is not a country. What country are you from?" She twirled her hair with one hand while closing her mysterious journal simultaneously.

I told her. She didn't believe me. People always think I am from a different country in Asia than I am from. Or they think I am Mexican. That makes me hungry for flan with chocolate.

"What's your name?" I asked, intrigued to find out more about this laughing girl.

"Iluj."

"That is a very unusual name."

"It's Hungarian. Are you hungry?" She started chuckling—that crazy accent—that mouth. She pulled out a box of chocolates, fished out the biggest one and reverently placed the box on the table. She indicated that I was invited to sit down.

I sat with her for over two hours and told her my stories. She liked most of my stories.

So, it all began with all of my serendipitous encounters with Herbert, Gary, and Iluj. My life back then started to be different. Yes, that August in 2014 was a turning point in hindsight, but hindsight is 20/20.

Enough about 2014 for now—back to the reality of 2040. Summoned downstairs, I went. Not before I grabbed a chocolate from the box I stash on the roof of the Empire State building—kind of where King Kong held the pretty blonde girl.

There it was, in the middle of the mahogany table in the living room. The pink box. A shadow dancing across it made it look like a dark, pastel pink.

As Gary tilted it, my smart phone from 2014 danced out of the box along with hard copies of the prints of all eighty eight women I had been involved with. Accented by a handwritten bio for each of them and pictures of us together. Usually kissing.

Herbert was standing right behind Gary and started laughing so hard he had to hold on to the broom.

Iluj gushed, "There you are! We wanted to start the party, but not without you. Ha ha ha ha ha ha."

Gary's voice was still very high and gay. "Come on kids! Gather round here. Let's look at the pretty pictures!" Gary enthusiastically gestured for them to gather around the table.

The children came; two boys and two girls. They

looked like they were a combination of Gary, Herbert, and Iluj, with a dash of myself. But that's what happens to family, doesn't it? They all blend together. You sacrifice non-conformity for love, when you need it.

The children's laughter filled the room and kept getting louder. More and more photographs, both from the smartphone and hard copies, fell onto the table like leaves falling from a tree.

I have learned that there are many different kinds of love.

Timed Out

"Nat, got a minute?" George's voice was breathing heavily on my purple cell phone.

"Maybe. What for?" I scratched my nose. (No picking, lol!) But, I was curious; George is unpredictable.

"To get your mind blown." He snickered. I chomped on my candy. Yummy for my tummy...maybe.

"Um. No, thanks. I rather like my mind. I think I'll keep it the way it is." I laughed. Ha ha ha!

I usually laugh fast and preemptively at ALL my jokes. Most of the time? Ha ha! This usually makes George get to the point tout suite. Or fast. Whichever.

"I don't care. I'm going to blow it."

"Ewwwwww! George!"

"What?"

"Nevermind. Continue, my silly boy."

I kept my sigh to myself. Honestly.

"Meet me at Starbucks in an hour."

"Is that a request or a demand?"

"Why would I demand YOU?"

"I don't know. Why would you?"

"Why should I think about that? Waste of thinking."

"Yeah. Sure. Waste."

Eye roll. But the eye roll was wasted because he couldn't see me. Phones are great but facial expressions are still lost. And farts. Most of the time, at least. Ha ha!

"Utter waste. Exactly."

He paused for a second.

"So, see you there."

"One hour?"

"No. Now it is 50 minutes. You've wasted ten minutes talking about nothing."

"49 minutes and counting! See ya!"

I hung up. Tout suite. This better be good. But, knowing George, it will be. He's quite brilliant. Lovable little bastard.

It would be really funny if there were a clock counting down all of the remaining minutes aloud until our meeting, like the voice over countdown scenes from movies—one of my favorite such scenes is from *Spaceballs*, a Mel Brooks comic extravaganza. I've actually never seen all of the Star Wars movies (gasp). This brings George paroxysms of terror, so I continue to eschew any viewings. It's so much fun to vex George.

The countdown scene in *Spaceballs* is awesome— Mega Maid's bust preceded by a very courteous female voice who says to the characters (while counting down their doom): "Have a nice day!" Not that meeting George is synonymous with the destruction of a fictional spaceship. Or, is it?

Regardless, I tempted fate by getting ready and making my way to our rendezvous at one of my favorite places. Just walking in is amazing. Did I say amazing? I meant exquisite. Resplendent. Euphoric. Yes. REALLY. It's *that* good. The aroma as you walk in...ah. Just breathe in that blessed scent. It's like none other. Always brings to mind brisk Fall mornings, steam rising from the mug, cream making pretty patterns as it's poured in...euphoria is almost not strong enough to describe my pleasure.

Oftentimes, simply waltzing in brings me to my Happy Place. This is before I've even slurped a sip; Joy! To George and the world.

Starbucks is a Utopia where rainbows erupt from every ray and serenity enters the soul on whispery wings of satisfaction and contentment. I glided to Starbucks on a miniature white pony singing, "My Favorite Things," from *The Sound of Music*. I already knew what I was going to order: a grande pumpkin spice latte. With dollops of extra creamy whipped cream, served by, "I am just like the bartender in that TV Show, *Cheers*, everyone doesn't know your name, but I-Barista do." Heaven is a place on earth. Heaven dances in circular motions in my cup. Lo-Carb, non-fat, sugar-free, and organic...not.

George knows about my coffee addiction (or, more accurately, obsession). It's hard to be my friend and *not* know. Especially a friend as close as George.

I walked in. But where was curious George? A bevy of people were lined up like contestants in *The Hunger Games*, waiting for their magic, life-sustaining elixir. Whoever invented coffee...he or she is my hero. Actually, I should find out to whom I owe my debt of gratitude. Or is it depth? I can send their descendants flowers every month. Or year. Or...decade. Whichever. Or maybe a really nice card. Like from Papyrus. Those cards are awesome. I could also write it with a really cool, navy-blue, British, pen.

Maybe I'll get one of those Venetian glass old-style styluses that use liquid ink from a jar. You know, the ones they sell at Barnes and Noble, usually promoted around Valentine's Day, with a heart wax seal and red ink included. Of course, I've always wanted to get one of those kits but never felt it was justified. Maybe, now, I have an excuse to get one. Done deal!

George, for all his hemming and hawing about punctuality, was late. I decided to get my latte and sneak in a scone (blueberry) before he could come and nab any bites. I also chose a seat next to one of their coffee displays; perhaps adorable Georgie Porgie would be inspired to buy me some coffee for my birthday (a belated present...he hadn't gotten me anything, yet). During our conversation I can subtly hint that ground coffee is very yummy and doesn't that bag over there look scrumptious?

Perfect. May work? Fingers crossed.

"Nat!!"

Oh God! When did he get here?? I put my hand to my chest, pulse racing.

"George! Don't *do* that!"

I gasped again, still trying to recover.

"Don't do what?"

George sat down and placed his steaming black coffee on the table. He looked a little disheveled. His silky, thick black hair was uncombed, his tie askew, and his five o'clock shadow hovered over four unidentifiable stains on his button-down shirt. I glanced at the floor as he swung his feet under the table and noticed that he was wearing mismatched socks, too—one black, one turquoise—under his brown penny loafers. He definitely was not looking like himself.

"Don't sneak up on me like that! I almost had a

heart attack!"

"Don't exaggerate. You are too young to have a heart attack."

"It's an expression."

"Well, don't express it."

Grrr! George is so vexing!

"George, why am I here? And, what happened to you?"

"What?" He looked down at himself. I pointed to the stains on his shirt and to his hair and lastly to his mismatched socks. He shrugged.

"Oh, that. Leave it. I have something awesome to tell you."

"What?" With George, you have to roll with the punches. If you try to attach yourself to any one line of questioning, he will annoy you to no end. He bops around topics like a squirrel leaps from tree to tree; he judges the so-called worth of a topic and if it doesn't warrant more thought than he thinks is necessary, he moves on. Game over in a nanosecond.

It's like having a conversation with that character from *50 First Dates*, 10-second-Tom; if you don't move on with him, you are left in the dust.

"You remember that movie you forced me to go see with you?"

"What movie?"

"*Zombie Love Clock*."

"I did not force you to see that! You wanted to come!"

"You pitched it as a tech movie. I was going to walk out of the theater after five minutes. But they had Peanut M&Ms at the concessions."

He took a sip of his coffee after blowing on it briefly.

"I would have killed you if you had left."

"True. But I would have been justified. You misrepresented it."

"George. I saw you. You liked it."

"I was pretending."

He tried to pull off a straight face, but his eyes twinkled.

"Liar." I grinned.

"Why would I lie?" He deadpanned.

"To save face," I said.

"Whatever. You remember it."

I rolled my eyes.

"Of course."

"I *did* it." He emphasized did. I had no idea what he was talking about.

"Did what?"

"I made one."

"A zombie love clock?? What???"

"Yes. I made a zombie love clock."

What???

"Does it work?" I was so incredulous.

"Yes."

No way!

"How do you know? It's not possible. You can't possibly have made one."

"I did. And I tested it. With humans and not zombies."

We both started to laugh. That George—he is so cute—I mean...annoying.

In case you are wondering, or haven't seen *Zombie Love Clock*, it's about being able to put a "Love Clock" in your wrist that will countdown to the exact second that you will meet your soul mate—one true love—Prince Charming, etc. It reads your hormone levels or something and somehow connects those who have "Love Clocks" to his or her match. If your ideal mate doesn't have a clock, your clock will not turn on until he or she gets one.

I'm not too clear on how exactly the clock is supposed to figure out who your soul mate is, but, it's also a *movie*. It doesn't work in REAL life!

"George. I hate to say it. But...I'm sorry. I don't believe you. It is just not possible to program true love. So, what did you do?"

"I can't tell you."

"Why?"

"It's too complicated. I'll show you."

"And, what do you mean, you 'tested it'? How?"

"I can't explain. I'll show you."

If you haven't figured it out already, George and I are very close. We are best buddies. We have gone through some very interesting adventures together (namely, Mr. Anon Guy incident, which I have talked about a lot; there may even be a published version of it...wink, wink.).

But, I have to tell you, I did not believe George had made a "Love Clock" or that it worked. However, he convinced me that he *thought* he had. And, maybe, sometimes, thinking makes it so.

He showed me his prototype an hour later; he was late getting to heaven on Earth because he had to drive over from his lab. I had biked over so I put my bike on the rack on George's car (he put it there two years ago, after he realized that I bike everywhere and sometimes it is awkward to ride in a car with a huge bike stuffed inside). His car is a jalopy. It's also insanely neat. I don't know how he manages to keep it so clean; you'd think, from the outside (dents everywhere, some sizable patches of rust and a droopy undercarriage) that the inside would be as dilapidated as the outside. But, somehow, he manages to keep it sparkling.

That's a miracle, in and of itself. Minus this "Love Clock" delusion he was under.

I walked in expecting, well, to be disappointed. I mean, come on. It's a total pipe dream; a piece of equipment that will tell you when you've met your soul mate? Attached to your wrist? Reading your hormone spikes? Yeah, right.

Also, how people think an algorithm will match them up is beyond me. If you ask me, all it takes is old fashioned chemistry. Yeah, chemistry. As in, see him or her from across a crowded room, take the plunge, and see if you both come out the other side ready to take on the world together.

Regardless, I wasn't expecting anything. So, to be completely honest, what happened was magical. And intense. And completely surprising. I know, I'm sorry. Enough with the knowing adjectives. I digress.

George showed me his workshop (again, freakishly clean); I hadn't been there in a few weeks and it seemed like the house elves from *Harry Potter* had cleaned. Every sparkling surface was dust-free, from the tops of the monitors to the coils of wires winding around everything like a giant dragon snake in a Chinese New Year's parade.

His lab reminds me of a bed of mating, multicolored snakes; all tangled together and fusing their respective information to make the next generation. iPhone 6 plus is coming out soon, by the way. Or may already be here, by the time you read this.

In the middle of one of the spotless counters was a smartwatch. At least, at first glance, that is what it appeared to be. And it looked very smart, indeed, all black and sleek. It would look good with a Givenchy ball gown, and that's saying something.

I was compelled by some force (perhaps curiosity) to get a closer look. And, even, to put it on. George's face was unreadable.

"Where'd you get this?"

"I told you. I made it."

George's face was suffused with pride.

"How?" I'm pretty sure my face was advertising confusion. And trepidation. George may have finally fallen off the deep end.

"How do you think? I bought the parts and put it together."

"George, you don't know how to make a watch."

I stated the obvious as I saw it.

"Clearly, you are wrong. I made that."

He pointed to the watch I was caressing absentmindedly, just like I had done with my fingers that time George and I had kissed. The only time.

"How does it work?" I looked for a power button to push to turn it on, but couldn't see anything.

"Here. I'll show you."

He started to walk over to me and all of a sudden, it started to beep. He lifted his left arm and I caught a glimpse of an identical "Love Clock" on his wrist. He got closer and the decibel and frequency of the watch's beeping increased tenfold. George took one more step and his own watch started to beep.

"George?! What's happening?!"

He stopped, completely surprised, and didn't move an inch. His face froze. It seemed like forever until he finished crossing the room to gently cup my hand and look at both of the alarming watches.

This whole time, they were screaming and beeping and going berserk. Later, I would realize that George had actually activated a panic button remotely (of course George had tricked me...he is such a good liar). He pretended that he had no idea what was going on. He looked down at his own beeping watch with a look of utter incredulity (he does look adorable when he plays the clueless boy!)

He picked up my wrist and held it close to his nose, studying the watch with an intensity strong enough to burn the midday sun. He surreptitiously put his fingers on a pressure point on my wrist used to (I know now) alleviate insomnia (among other things), but which, previously, he had told me was used to calm people down. Or something like that, I don't know.

In any case, my heart rate slowed (effects of my delusion that he was pressing a point to calm me) and my breaths started to synchronize with his. Knowing the plot of the movie would be helpful, at this point (whenever the "Love Clock" beeps crazily, it means you have found "the One"). I blame it on my romanticism, but I was actually falling for it. I thought the "Love Clock" on my wrist was telling me that I had met my "One"...aka George. And that his own watch was telling him that he had met his ONE. THE ONE. Moi.

He stared into my eyes and I had flashbacks to all of the years we had been friends and everything that we had done together. I saw each memory in a new light. As if I were seeing them through George's eyes. And that he had loved me from the very start, though I had been unaware. Or, at least, consciously unaware. Unconsciously, I may have picked up his subtle signals and refused to acknowledge them, and, therefore, was blind to them.

In that moment, I became cognizant of how very close he was standing, how his eyes were almost melting into mine, and it seemed like the most natural thing in the world to lean closer and meet his lips as they came toward mine.

Unlike a previous kiss we had shared, this one was passionate and intense. All of a sudden, his arms were around me (don't forget, the "Love Clocks" were still beeping throughout all of this) and my arms were around him and I was pressed up against him so close I could feel the buttons on his shirt through mine and his belt buckle on my stomach. Exactly where our tongues were and how our lips were moving is private, thank you very much.

But, it was life changing. For sure. I had never shared such a kiss with anyone.

I had never kissed anyone as *close* to me as George.

Usually, my dates were with complete strangers; random men who had asked me out at a bar or café. The kisses came after a few glasses of wine at dinner on the third or fourth date. Though those were pleasant, I didn't realize how a kiss backed by so much history would feel. It was as if I had woken up and finally seen the color of the sky for the first time. As if I had experienced the sky for my whole life but had never seen it's color. Until right then.

Heady. To say the least.

George is telling me as I jot this down that he had been planning this set up ever since we had seen the movie together. He had realized its potential and knew that he could take advantage of my gullibility. I am really quite gullible. He's right.

Ahem. In any case, I didn't find out until a month later that the "Love Clocks" were, in fact, fake. Just two tripped out smart watches that George could remotely set off.

I felt so disappointed.

He told me eventually only because I kept telling him that he would make billions of dollars if he marketed the clocks. He broke it to me gently, but I still can't believe I had actually believed he had done it.

I had tried to be skeptical, but—alakazam!—at some magical point, I was too invested. I believed him. And, in that moment of believing, my turquoise eyes saw the color of the sky. I couldn't go back to life before, afterward.

For better or worse, I am in love with *my* own *George* (and, in case you missed it, George is the first name of Mr. Knightly from *Emma*). Serious, crazy, and completely-in-love-with-me, George.

It just goes to show, even the best minds can be fooled by remotes. Or hormones. Or both.

PART II

FALLS

"...Between the idea
And the reality
Between the motion
And the act
Falls the Shadow..."

T. S. Eliot, *The Hollow Men*

Three Hundred and Three

Her hands are soapy with suds; they've escaped the murky waters and are up to her elbows. She's careful to keep her white silk blouse as far from the lip of the sink as her reach allows. Bacon grease swirls and French Vanilla granules ride the eddies she creates, her arms at the center of each whirlpool. The early morning light sneaks underneath half-drawn blinds and provides a muted glow to her stainless steel kitchen. She loves this time to herself; a calm moment she cherishes, after breakfast is killed and before the day begins.

Where is her family? She's not sure; the kids are silent. You could hear a pebble drop. A bit too quiet, isn't it? She starts to lift her right hand but catches herself just in time and resists the urge to scratch her forehead. Imagine the splatter that would have caused, and to her pristine top, too! She sighs and is just about to call out to her husband, the words forming on her lips...then it hits her: today is the *eleventh*!

In her haste to leave her family's apartment, 175A,

she neglects to put on her favorite crimson scarf. As she runs to the elevator bank, she feels naked. She clutches at the pale skin of her exposed sunburned and bruised neck with her beringed left hand as she stuffs her new keyring into her worn Marc Jacobs purse.

It's going to bother her. The scarf. She berates herself a million ways as she starts to zoom down. Floor 175 to ground zero. The elevator is fast, but it still takes a little while to descend that distance. She experiences sharp pangs of self-reproof with each stroke of her red and purple skin as she watches herself in the elevator mirror. Her husband is not going to like it, either. But, there's no chance she could make it to the apartment and back down in time for the drawing. She has to be there; her Hermes anniversary scarf must stay behind. No crimson.

The floors ding slowly. She breathes heavily from her mad rush to the elevator. *Just another manic Tuesday*. She straightens her pencil skirt and checks her thigh highs for any tears. She's presentable, though sticky; dawn residue is trapped between her fingers and under the bands of her Tiffany solitaire and diamond eternity rings. It itches. Sweat forms at the base of her spine and slowly dribbles down.

She wonders if they've started without her. But, how could they? There are certain rules to follow. Certain traditions. She's not clear on all of them, but she's certain of a few; she ticks them off as she remembers them on her fingers. The elevator whines and dings in tandem.

One: All residents must be present and have a ticket; no exceptions.
Two: All drawings are to be held at 8:46 AM, the

11th of the month.

Three: All drawings continue until a Winner is announced.

Four: All Winners are final; no redrawings.

Five: All Winners are announced by the Officiant.

Six: All Officiants serve until they win.

She's aware of a few more traditions, but if she's honest with herself, she hasn't paid too much attention to them. She undoubtedly looks forward to the drawings, however. She can't deny that they add a certain touch of spice to life; the prolonged suspense, the sense of unity, the adrenaline rush...

She huffs and sweats out of the elevator, goddamn broken air conditioning. Again! Her heels clack across the marble floor. She flings her bag over her shoulder and swings her hips as she waddles in her too-tight skirt out the double glass doors.

The dense downtown Manhattan air surrounds her and her red hair curls instantaneously in the 125 degree (99% humidity) heat. Hot day for a Winner, isn't it? She squints in the morning light and squares her shoulders. She turns left and runs toward Ground Zero.

As she approaches the back of the crowd, she stretches her neck then immediately retracts it. Pain lances through her damaged skin. She looks up and feels a tinge of embarrassment as she meets the eyes of Mr. McGruff; he's never late for anything. Let alone a Drawing. She wants to look away from him but she doesn't want to admit that she almost forgot the date. Almost forgot to show up. She covers her exposed neck with her free hand.

She keeps her gaze steady and lifts up the left corner of her mouth, in a mock-smile.

"Mr. McGruff, good morning."

"Mornin'. A bit late, aren't ya?"

She blushes and forces a smile. Shrugging, she grips her purse against her shoulder.

"I had to finish the dishes in the sink."

Her excuse falls flat. And sounds made up. He looks her up and down as if to say, 'Doing dishes in *that* outfit?'

She keeps her chin up. *So what?* He quirks an eyebrow at her.

"Your husband will be missing you, surely."

Her eyes narrow and she grips her neck tighter. She oozes equanimity—remain calm and eat cake?

"Do you happen to know where he is in the crowd?"

"I think, up at the front," he growls. "Over to the left...there!" *Stupid elitist, non-conformist trophy wife*, McGruff's face says. She can read it clear as day.

He points and she follows his hand with her blue eyes, trying to see past the crowd of 303 residents, gathered amongst the ruins of the Twin Towers.

She catches a glimpse of her husband's frowning face. He seems tense. He scans the back of the crowd, searching for her like a lost poodle looking for its owner.

She raises her hand and waves. He catches the movement and their eyes meet. He's pissed. He jerks his head quickly at her. She half-stops a quick gulp of air.

"Excuse me," she clears her throat, "my husband is waiting for me. Thank you for pointing him out to me."

"Yup." He turns away from her, focusing instead on the new Officiant, Mr. Aite, up front.

She makes her way through the assembly, picking up bits and pieces of conversations as she passes her building's residents.

"Is it going to be like last time, Mommy?"

"Sort of, honey. A new winner will be chosen."

"Will it be me?"

"There's no use in speculating, sweetheart. We'll know soon enough."

"What if it's me?"

She turns her head and misses the mother's response. She thinks they live in 26A, but she isn't quite sure. She thinks sure rhymes with pure.

Her heart flutters and she gasps for a breath. The suspense of who will win has always made her pulse race faster than a subway leaving Times Square.

No matter how many drawings she's been to (and she's lost count) it always affects her the same way. Pulse hammering, sweat beading, hands shaking, nerves jangling. Every time.

She passes by two older Saudi Arabian women from the third floor, standing behind their husbands.

"I heard that Mr. Aite is new to the concept of the drawing." Mrs. "I'm-So-Perfect" reveals this information like a cat proffering a mouse to its owner.

"What? That's unheard of." Mrs. Black's voice registers shock to the tenth power.

"My husband swears it. He heard it from Mr. Belial."

"Well, I don't know where he could have come from. We've always had a drawing. Always. It's tradition."

Her breath stops as she listens to the two women as she passes. Can it be true? No drawing? Where? She scratches her nose and almost bumps into the back of Mrs. "I'm-So-Perfect"; a woman who thinks the world revolves around her and her perfect Navy Seal husband, perfect blonde hair, perfect Israeli accent, and perfect life.

She clasps her neck, killing for her scarf, catches

her breath and scoots around the impeccably dressed, coiffed and cultured Mrs. Imogen Hightower. Ironic name, that, considering she and her husband live on the 3rd floor.

"Sorry," she mutters. Mrs. Black, standing next to her 3rd floor neighbor, bobs her head at her instead before turning back to Imogen. Imogen doesn't even bother to look at her. She continues her speculations uninterrupted.

"I wonder if anyone else knows. I can't imagine where he must have grown up." Imogen appears only slightly bemused. She could be discussing this week's IN nail polish color, for all of the care she displays.

"No drawing where he's from? You can't be serious. You just can't be." Mrs. Black sounds as scandalized as a Catholic priest in Boston. Blasphemous! No drawing!?

But, if there weren't one...

If wishes were dreams...

She is unable or unwilling to finish her thought. Ludicrous! Mrs. Black is right; there is no use thinking of THAT; there has always been a drawing here. Wherever Mr. Aite is from, it must be a long way off. Maybe New Jersey? On the 11th day, HE said, above all else, conformity.

Her husband beckons to her again and she jogs faster. As she gets closer, she notices a newly piled set of stones. She considers the leftmost rock, wondering how heavy it is. It looks huge. Bigger than any rubble she's seen piled in the square before. At least, after September 12, 2001. Monstrous.

The specters of the Twin Towers rise out of what little rubble remains, the memorial long since crumbled and broken from wind, weather and time. Occasionally, she can spot a surviving plaque or two, indicating the solemn news of the fate of the Towers on the eleventh of September, all those years ago. It's an interesting place to hold the monthly drawings; it reminds her of the city's history. And the inhabitants' spirit.

Her husband extends his hand out to her as she finally reaches him. "She's here, Mr. Aite. She's here, now."

He clamps his hand around her forearm and squeezes. The lines around his mouth betray his strain. She'll hear about this later, that's for sure. Her hand slips a bit on her neck as she gulps again.

"Finally made it, huh?" Mr. Aite jokes.

The residents around her start laughing. She looks at her husband. He notices her hand and the lack of her scarf. Oops. She turns away from his glare.

She hesitates but, nonetheless, a smile forms on her lips. Better sell it.

"Had to clear the sink. Can't leave those dishes by themselves, they'll create all kinds of havoc on their own, especially if I win." She musters a chuckle and surprises herself with how authentic it sounds.

She gets a good laugh from Mr. Aite. Their new Officiant. He was chosen after the last drawing, his predecessor having won on that particular morning. His brown hair is longer than most everyone else's; he lives on the 93rd floor and has a tabby cat. He's pretty young for an Officiant; only 33. She looks at his biceps, showing through his white t-shirt, and can't help but appreciate their bulk. *Does he find me attractive? How could I know?*

She would only barely be able to touch her fingertips together if she were to wrap her hands around either upper arm. Impressive. He must make women younger than her melt at the slightest smoldering glance. Hell, she would melt if he ever passionately glanced at her.

He carries the coffer housing the tickets, all 303 of them. Every man, woman and child will take one, older siblings helping younger ones, if necessary. And only one will be the Winner.

The laughter dies abruptly. Fade to black. Mr. Aite clears his throat. He rings the bell. The makeshift dais quivers from the impact. Boom! "Everyone here? Anyone missing?"

His deep bass vibrates through the people like a wave. People turn this way and that to check on their neighbors. Most tend to stand by floor, neighbors next to neighbors, so it's easy to tell when someone is missing. No one raises an alarm and it seems that everyone is accounted for.

Mr. Aite rings his bell a second time.

"Very well. As it is quite hot already, we will get started. I'm sure everyone is anxious to get out of this heat. As you know, our building was designed with two apartments per floor, so we will start with the first floor, apartment 1A, and proceed through all of the floors until we reach apartment 175A."

She shuffles her feet (*What if he kissed me? What would I do? Would I pull away? Or kiss back?*), and notices her neighbor, Claudia, fidgeting as well. This is always the boring part of the event; the reading of the rules. Her thoughts and eyes drift as he continues his spiel. Yada, yada, yada!

"Each resident in each apartment will take a ticket, youngest to oldest. No one will open theirs until everyone has taken one."

She notices a perfectly round pebble next to her husband's foot; she leans down and picks it up. Its cool, smooth surface contrasts starkly with her hot, sweaty hands. She passes it back and forth, grateful to have something to play with. The air hits her hurting neck and she wishes once again for her scarf.

She looks to her left and sees her two little devils. Her kids are both sitting on the gravel next to her husband, their heads together as they whisper. She smiles as Benjamin makes a cup with his hand over Bethany's ear, tells her something hilarious, then receives his own cupped joke from her in return.

She sees other kids, from toddlers to teenagers, milling about or quietly playing, waiting for the action to start.

"As one, we will open our tickets and the Winner will step forward. Once the Winner has identified him or herself, I will collect all of the papers back in the Drawing Coffer, starting with apartment 175A. The Winner will wait in front of the dais and keep his or her ticket until everyone else has handed in theirs."

Mr. Aite wipes some sweat off his brow before continuing. "I will then take the ticket from the Winner and ring my bell to officially signal the end of the Drawing. The Winner will then remain standing at the front to receive the Prize."

The residents squirm in the 125 degree heat and a beat of silence ripples through the air like a viper in a grassy African field.

Mr. Aite looks out at the crowd. "Any questions?"

"Nah, we know the drill."

She doesn't recognize the young voice, but he sounds impatient.

"Yeah, let's get to it!"

The second teenage boy guffaws, eager to get started and to hear the results. She can't make out their faces, but she sees them standing next to Ms. Cephas, from 69B. They must be the 69A boys; 15

and 17. She shifts her weight.

Mr. Aite rings his bell a third time.

"Alright, then. Apartment 1A."

She sees ancient Mr. Eder step out of the crowd. His wooden cane clunks with each step he takes, the rubberized sole long since worn through. His wife won the drawing two years ago. His hand shakes as he circles and approaches a ticket. He tucks it in his back pocket and moves aside.

"1B."

Ms. Gossip steps up to the box, pauses, then reaches in and picks one. Ms. Gossip is known as the loose-lipped queen of the century. Or, she should be.

The heat bears down on her aching neck as she grasps the pebble more firmly in her hand. Unforgiven. She fans her face with her free hand, her fingers still sticky. Wafts of Dawn's signature fragrance greet her nostrils. The scent brings her back to the morning, when she had been content and happy to be on her own in front of the sink, a lazy day ahead of her. Until she remembered the date.

"2A."

Mr. Aite calls out the empty apartment number, even though everyone is aware it's uninhabited. Something about ghosts from the planes dancing around 2A. A new tenant hasn't yet come.

"2B."

"3A." ... "10B." ... "33A." ... "61B." ... "72A."

She watches one of her reading club members, Elisabeth, stride forward to claim her stub.

They've been reading, "The Great Gatsby," by F. Scott Fitzgerald. She left her copy on the nightstand. She loves Daisy and can't stand Daisy's husband. Elisabeth suggested the book and everyone has eaten it up, unlike, "Far From the Madding Crowd," by

Thomas Hardy. That one was a bit tough to get into; she had liked it, but Drusilla thought it sucked.

Those discussions had been painful to stomach. Drusilla is one of those people who always has an opinion, and usually a very strong one, about everything. It might have something to do with her awful name. What an unfortunate name to have. She has never heard Drusilla's opinion on the drawing, though. What would Drusilla say about Mr. Aite's unusual, drawing-free background?

They've never discussed the drawing. It seems to be the one thing that is never mentioned. She never talks about it to her husband or her kids; she doesn't gossip about the Winner...she seems to collectively ignore everything to do with the drawing. Rule number 111 of the drawing, you never talk about the drawing? Why?

Is it...because she's apprehensive? Will it change how her husband talks to her? He already has discussions with her about what **he** deems to be her flaws. He smirks at her male friends whenever he sees them—his jealousy dancing through the air—even though he has plenty of female friends himself (some of them might even be his mistresses)—and *she* never browbeats *him* about them. She wonders if he is amorous with them?

She sees the next resident take a ticket and wonders about those little slips of paper...wonders if it would make life better if her husband ever won. Her neck twinges with pain; she puts her hand on it to protect her hot, swollen skin. Her skin peels off, some blisters forming. Those came suddenly. It must be the heat. God, is this Manhattan or the deserts of Afghanistan?!

Their marriage of 9 years, eleven months, has been

a struggle since day one; her parents always hated him. Her parents won the drawing back to back; that had been a remarkable occurrence. Hardly any married couples had won the drawing back to back; her parents are written on a record somewhere. She's sure of it. She vaguely recalls it may be by the memorial fountains on Ground Zero.

Her Tuesday running partner smiles at her and she realizes that Mr. Aite must have called out 95A. That means her number is up soon.

Time flies, especially when you don't think you want it to. Or aren't paying attention.

She looks around at the gathered assembly; those who already have their tickets stand up straighter, look more tense and are generally more subdued. Those waiting to be called still have an air of laziness about them, as if they could be standing in line for something as banal as a cappuccino. The closest high-end coffee chain, Cuppa Joe, is only a stone's throw from the square.

"98B."

Old Mrs. Gomer looks like her bones are all welded together; her legs and arms are so rigid it's a wonder she can move forward at all. She's one of the skinniest of all the inhabitants, but it's a toss up whether her bark is worse than her bite or vice versa. She seems to have a vile thing to say about everyone and everything.

The only time she's ever smiled is at the conclusion of a drawing. Her smile is almost akin to the grin of a wolf or the look on a cat's face when playing with its dinner.

Frighteningly happy.

"101A."

Her adrenaline levels spike. Her breath comes in

fast little gasps now, as if she is still running, still late to the drawing, still hustling along the litter-strewn street, the pavement throwing off waves of heat like a hairdryer set to low.

She wonders if anyone ever died of a heat stroke while waiting for a ticket. Maybe she will be the first one. That would make a cool headline in the NY Post! She shifts from her right foot to her left and tries to take her arm away from her husband; he is still grasping it. Hard. So hard, you can see the blood, just under the surface.

Her husband finally speaks to her. "What?" His tone seethes with undisguised contempt.

"I'm hot." His eyebrows go up then down.

"Why were you late?" He keeps a hold of her arm, not letting her get away, as if that will make up for her late arrival this morning.

"I'm hot." She says again.

He hesitates then releases her arm. There are five large red marks on her arm.

"Wow. Look." He doesn't bother, even though she lifts up the marks to show him what he's done.

"We'll talk about this later."

She shudders. What if there is no later? What if she gets heat stroke right now and keels over?

He doesn't care. She could die today and it wouldn't bother him.

At least, her pettiness tells her that he wouldn't. He hasn't been affectionate towards her in weeks. She wonders if he's sleeping with the frisky woman in 77B. She's seen them together and not known who was flirting more, the woman or her husband.

She pretends that it doesn't hurt, like walking safely over sharp rocks, but the pain slithers into her consciousness.

Maybe Ms. Frisky from 77B will win. Wouldn't that be something. Thou shalt not covet thy neighbor's...cat. She finds this hilarious but restrains her impending laughter.

She holds onto that thought as 103A is called out. Her neighbor, Mr. Stone. His wife won the drawing 10 years ago and their daughter won it last year. He looks down at his ticket. His face has an indecipherable expression. Does he want to win, too?

She tries to stop herself speculating, but it's hard not to, at this stage in the game. Almost everyone has gotten a slip.

"175A."

She catches her breath. Her daughter, the youngest, steps up first, her brother right behind her. The drawing is by age, youngest to oldest. She will go after them. Bethany picks one up in 0.93 seconds and hops back over. Bethany takes her hand that is grasping the round pebble and attempts to pry it out; she holds onto it as long as she can before letting Bethany have it. Bethany's eyes light up as a smile is drawn on her face. Bethany clutches her prize with pride.

She sees Benjamin leave the dais from the corner of her eyes. NOW. It's now. She knows. It's her turn.

She steps up to the wooden coffer, its scarred edges faded and worn. How old is it? She can't remember when the drawings started. She learned about it at school, but those dates have since vanished from her mind like the Twin Towers from the New York landscape.

There are only two tickets left. Two slips of paper. One is all of the way at the right-most edge of the box and the other is near the middle. She puts her hand in, intending to take the one in the middle, but her hand surprises her by grasping the one by the edge of the box instead. She can't put it down, again, either; You touch it, You take it.

She swallows her disappointment; she wanted the one in the middle. What possessed her to take the other one? Nerves? Or was it something else?

She steps back and her husband pushes past her to take the slip of paper that she wanted. She huffs and hunches her shoulders slightly.

"Wonderful. Everyone has a ticket. Now, as one, let's open our tickets. Three, two, one!"

She opens her hand and looks down. Her ticket is not blank, this time. It has something written on it. In red ink. She looks up in a daze. Her heart is in her throat. Frogs have hopped two-by-two down her spine. She is the Winner.

She feels as if she is underwater. Her movements are slow, her ears are stopped up. As if in a dream, she hands her purse to her husband, walks forward and takes her place in front of the dais. The red letters blink across her vision, faster and faster. The Winner. The Winner. The Winner. Like the neon sign over Cuppa Joe's window display.

Time has stopped. She looks out at the faces of her neighbors and can't help but think, *Is this it? Really? Is this happening? It can't be. I'm the Winner??*

She watches in silence as the Officiant gathers the other tickets, the losing tickets. The drawing process reverses, each person stepping forward to put their discarded tickets in the box. It goes faster than she thinks is possible. In reality it takes 102 minutes.

She doesn't look at her husband. She can't look at him. She can't look at her kids, either. Sweat jets off her and her feet feel rooted to the ground. Her ticket is like a limp noodle in her sticky palm. Her Dawn-coated fingers are glued together.

Then, the Officiant turns to her and says, "Okay, let me see."

She opens her fingers with an effort, and shows him her ticket. It's a Winner.

He takes it from her and rings his bell a fourth time.

"We have a Winner, everyone. I now declare Operation "S" a go. It's time for us to mete out her Prize."

His voice sounds somber and joyful at the same time. He is young. And he's a loser. It's his second time at a drawing. She looks at him and sees his eyes gleaming with anticipation. He looks at her and sees only a Winner.

She gulps. Her breaths come faster and faster. She's hyperventilating. She sees her son reach down and pluck a stone from the pile nearest him. The sight paralyzes her.

His name forms on her mouth, as if she could tell him to put it down. *Benjamin, do not even think of throwing that.* Her lips open wide, she takes in a gasp of air and just as she's about to scream, a rock hits her hard in the mouth.

"Bullseye!" One of the 69A boys laughs in ecstasy. Tears spurt from her eyes. She reaches up to hold her mouth and another rock catches her in the ear. Tears blind her as pain shoots over her scalp.

"Alright, alright, everyone. Let's be quick about it now." Mr. Aite takes aim. His biceps bulge. She puts her arms out in front of her in a silent plea, her mouth full of blood and her front teeth broken, begging with her eyes for someone to tell them all to stop, for them to think about it, she's their *neighbor*, but no one does.

A rock hits her squarely in the chest, and she falls down. She tries to shout, to scream, but her breath is knocked out. She opens her eyes. Her husband lurks above her. *My, what a big rock you have*...she moves her lips but no sound comes out. She sees his face light up. He is grinning like a circus clown. Time to get your prize. Ding, dong, ditch!

A bell rings for the fifth time.

"Well done, everyone. Have a great day! Don't forget to get your free organic latte at Cuppa Joe," Mr. Aite calls out and the residents waltz back towards Cuppa Joe. Must celebrate the hunt.

Mr. Aite takes the damp winning ticket off the dais and puts it in his pocket. He picks up the box and takes it with him as he starts to leave the square. The Drawing Coffer now contains 302.

She lies on the ground, oblivious. She lets herself go and starts falling. 11 seconds later her eyes hit the back of her head, resting on the gravel at Ground Zero. Dead on arrival. She IS the Winner.

Her name was Liberty.

Vacation Time

Everyone wants to believe their own delusions and lies. Bryan Vacation (yes, that was his real name; his Alabama, moved to Pennsylvania at 10, Baptist, fire and brimstone, here comes the Revelation, Beast, grandma named him) was just like you and me in that one, small way.

Bryan also fed our lusty demons and monsters—so, perhaps, in many other small, medium, and especially extra large ways—he was *a lot* like you and me. But, since all humans lie, we would lie about this. Vehemently. Especially to ourselves. And to other people who we claimed to love the most.

Bryan opened up the inexpensive Staples notebook and took out the $400 red checkered tie tucked neatly inside. The tie felt soft like the smoothly shaved underarms of Bryan's trophy blonde (from a former Soviet Republic, failed at modeling, only got an Extra role in an Angelina Jolie movie) girlfriend. He allowed himself a moment of tenderness and introspection. The moment was ephemeral, like all fleeting moments in our air-breathing existences. Bryan put his mask back on. One thing he learned early in his business is that you: **don't fuck with the brand**.

Indeed, Bryan Vacation was a good brand. An excellent brand. But things never turn out the way you expect them too...

2014 was a great year. But, that plain, Staples notebook was BIG. Really big. Lots of page views on the internet—lots of cash—tons of glory—and, most importantly, it offered a chance for people to see Bryan as the empathetic journalist/marketing superstar who cares more for the masses than for his bank account or his brand value. The contents of that notebook would herald a meteoric rise in Bryan Vacation's star. A star that would burn so bright, its light would be seen for many years after its inevitable death. A light so bright, the darkest black hole that followed it would retain afterimages, illusory palinopsia, hallucinatory palinopsia, ad infinitum, even about a hundred years later.

In 2014, Bryan had been the mastermind behind eight of the top ten Receipt Porn Stories. You know, like that one where the CoffeeStar barista had written on the latte cup, "Slitty-Chinky eyed woman." That was a tough one, because Bryan had to find the perfect half-Caucasian, half-Asian woman in The Mission neighborhood of San Francisco.

Finding either/or was relatively easy in The Mission, but finding the right combination (in Bryan's eyes—after all, Bryan's world, Bryan's rules) was as tough as finding a parking spot for a Jeep, Saturday at 7PM there (peak dinnertime, as people ate dinner on a Saturday night much earlier than they do in New York in The Mission).

But, Bryan *did* find Annette Wood. He thought her eyes looked Asian enough so that people would sympathize but she also looked very white.

Bryan paid the barista $100 and Annette another $100. The barista said, "Nothing personal. Asian people do have different eyes than we do." Later that night, the barista, Bryan, and her Asian boyfriend went out to dinner at the Cheesecake Factory and laughed about the whole incident over margaritas.

Annette blogged about this; she posted photos of the latte cup and wrote pages about how this was a traumatic incident for her.

Outrage exploded. Kablam!

People in 2014 America found it a lot easier to hide behind their smart phones, tablets, phablets, laptops, watches and Google glasses than to face real life. Instead, they created alternative lives for themselves. Moral lives. Outraged-at-how-she-was-treated lives.

Much easier, cleaner and more efficient to hide behind such an online alter ego than to deal with human emotions and nuances in the flesh. Or so the people of 2014 thought.

We all want very hard to believe our delusions and lies. If only wishes came true...

Millions of pageviews and free Oprah-Aresenio Hall publicity and tens of thousands of dollars in advertising revenues and endorsement offers later, that became one of the top Receipt Porn Stories of the year. Hell, Bryan was even able to get an apology and a lifetime unlimited money gift card from CoffeeStar's CEO. It sure beat writing stories for $50 or, on a good day, $200, as many of Bryan's struggling-journalist-friends were doing.

Lest we forget other infamous dealings Bryan had in 2014, there was the ISIS terrorist that Bryan paid $5,000 in cold hard cash to behead a British journalist and give Bryan and his newspaper, *The Manhattan*

Roast, an exclusive on the whole story. He easily made 10 times that amount of money back—and who cares about a beheading or two if it advanced Bryan's interests? After all, thousands died on 9/11.

But, then, there were the *fun* parts of the job for Bryan. Those days that made him feel like a kid again. His childhood was very painful and confusing. With many uncomfortable positions. One stand out day (not during his childhood, but in his adult years), a really superbly fun day, Bryan paid some Stanford and MIT guys, who were drinking Appletinis in a Palo Alto pub, $800 cash to hack naked pictures of celebrities, including that blonde from that Hungry Games (or something) series.

He was stoked that he got to see the pictures in advance. And masturbate to his heart's content. He imagined some freaky porn dialogue frothing out of her pink, pouty lips as he delved inside her red wonderland again and again and again. He imagined her moans escalating in pitch and sluttiness as he climaxed, her perky pink-and-white-targets just begging for his ammunition.

His copies might have gotten some actual droplets on them—which was all the hotter—since he had blown up a pic of her chest to an 8 by 11.

That day's bribe gave Bryan many thrills and the money was good. Really, really good. Lots of moolah flowing like the Hudson River flows into the Atlantic. Or like hot lava pulsing over hard rocks endlessly.

Bryan was a legend (mostly in his own mind) at *The Manhattan Roast*, the daily newspaper everyone read—but lied about reading—let alone liking. Kind of like internet porn. Bryan was adept at getting page—views and the much coveted advertising dollars on the paper's website. In 2014, it was a cliché to say newspapers were dying a slow death at the hands of the Herculean Internet. Trite but true.

Except, maybe newspapers were like zombies from that movie—their brains half chomped-out—roaming the streets for more pageviews and ad dollars, often stumbling. Who needs truth when you can have money?

Bryan had sandy blonde hair and aquamarine eyes. Eyes that never looked to Ithaca—237 miles Northwest on Route 80—where the river matched the highway, twist for twist. A college town. Pennsylvania. The kind of college town where drunk Amish kids would overturn their buggies next to the pub where the football players, coaches and their gang would guzzle cheap beers.

Ithaca State University—nicknamed Pennitentiary or Penn State due to the prison nearby—had the most winning football program...for what seemed like forever. Football brought big dollars to the school. Who cares about education and the students when you have so much money flowing through the athletic programs? Athletic programs were the Gods. Judge. Jury. And Executioner.

The university rationalized the lie that sports made men out of these student-athletes. They ignored the real numbers: the drop-outs; the graduates with no employable skills; the very small percentage who played 3rd string running back for the Rams (or other teams).

That was how it was. Their rules, their world. But, as you and I know, this changed 80 years later. The lynchpin? You guessed it—Bryan Vacation.

A wise man (Clint Eastwood or John Wayne) once said, "Life itself is a rationalization because eventually we will all die."

But—none of that mattered to Bryan. He had a night of wild sex to look forward to with Blondie. He (half-jokingly) called his girlfriend *Blondie*.

Sometimes, when she felt sunny and wild, she giggled at his jokes. Her eyes would light up and sparkle like fireworks launching from the East River on the Fourth of July. For just a moment. And Bryan loved to see his baby smile. But, dark clouds would cover her milky white face and steal her sunny disposition, smile and innocence. Just like the Russian troops, who snatched it away from Blondie as they beat and sodomized her on the streets of Kiev on the eve of the umpteenth Soviet squelching. Sad but true.

Bryan and Blondie were together, though, safe; two kids deeply in love in an angry, fucked-up-world-gone-wrong; they were living a teenage dream. They were lying to themselves. Perhaps deluding is a more accurate term. Willful deceit?

But, that night, after he got through the contents of the hotter-than-hot Staples notebook, he knew that they would be free. Everything would be good. So good, it would taste like a chocolate cake with whipped cream caressing the top. That night, they would have one of their four hour, marathon love-making sessions (Blondie was a practical girl; she hated "making-love"—she preferred fuck. Because a duck is a duck. Quack, quack).

Blondie's pretty Russian looks concealed a steely, detached and nihilistic interior. To her, morality was like chewing gum and could be stretched. So could the truth.

Blondie supported herself by working at a dentist's office—a good opportunity to meet doctors who she would fuck for free ass, boob and nose jobs. She also started a full-body massage spa on Madison avenue.

Blondie and her wannabe model friends—they complained about the low pay and exploitation in the modeling industry. They failed to understand that everyone has to negotiate for themselves in Capitalism (unless you can afford really good agents or lawyers). They would take off their tops, shake their tits and give massages and hand jobs to detectives and doctors (dicks'n'docs) for $200 per hour. They never crossed the line into full-blown sexual intercourse with their clients. That honor was reserved for their revolving door of boyfriends and sugar daddies. Bryan was a lucky guy indeed.

Bryan set aside the red checkered tie and opened the Staples notebook. His elixir. Philosopher's Stone. On the first page, he saw the start of the confession detailing the events that had taken place at Coach Sandski's apartment on the East Side. The Staples notebook he possessed had liquid gold inside of it. Liquid. Gold. Sandski's apartment was not too far away from Grand Central, where Blondie lived, Bryan noted to himself. The confession was only a few pages long. Still, Bryan could see dollar signs all over it. He knew it would be huge, even before the story broke. He knew he held dynamite in his hands.

It read:

True! True!—nervous—very, very dreadfully nervous I had been and am; but why will you say that I am mad? The disease sharpened my senses—not destroyed—not dulled them. Above all, my sense of hearing is very acute.

I heard all things in the heavens and on the earth. I heard many things in hell. How, then, can you say that am I mad? Listen to me! and observe how healthily—how calmly I can tell you the whole story.

It is impossible to say how first the idea entered my brain; but once conceived, it haunted me day and night. Object, there was none. Passion, there was none. I loved the coach Raterno—the old man. He never wronged me or insulted me. I had no desire for his fortune or his fame. I was a good Assistant Coach. Everyone knew me.

I also loved the boys. All the young boys. Why else do you think I would start, The Second Kilometer Charity? *To help those boys.*

I think it was his eye! yes, it was this! He had the eye of a vulture—a pale blue eye, with a film over it. Whenever it fell upon me, my blood ran cold; and so by degrees—very gradually—I made up my mind to take the life of the old man and rid myself of the eye! forever. This was right after the old man found out about the kids and me.

Now, this is the point. You think of me as mad. Madmen know nothing. But you should have seen me. You should have seen how wisely I proceeded—with what caution—with what foresight—with what dissimulation I went to work!

I was never kinder to the old man than during the whole week before I killed him.

And every night, about midnight, I turned the latch of his door and opened it—oh so gently! And then, when I had made an opening sufficient for my head, I put in a flashlight turned off and then I thrust in my head. Oh, you would have laughed to see how cunningly I thrust it in! I moved it slowly—very, very slowly, so that I might not disturb the old man's sleep. It took me an hour to place my whole head through the door so that I could see him as he lay upon his bed. Ha! would a madman have been so wise as this? And then, when my head was well in the room, I turned on the flashlight cautiously—oh, so cautiously—cautiously (for the button squeaked)—I shone it just so that a single, thin ray fell upon the vulture eye!

And this, I did this for seven long nights—every night just at midnight—but I found the eye! always closed; and so it was impossible to do the work; for it was not the old man who annoyed me, but his Evil Eye! And, every morning, when the sun came up, I went boldly into his room and spoke bravely to him, calling him by name in a hearty tone and inquiring how he had passed the night. So you see, he would have been a very canny old man, indeed, to suspect that every night, just at twelve, I looked in on him while he slept.

On the eighth night, I was more than usually cautious in opening the door. A watch's minute hand moves more quickly than did mine. Never before that night had I felt the extent of my own powers—of my sagacity.

I could scarcely contain my feelings of triumph. To think that, there I was, opening the door, little by little, and he not even to dream of my secret deeds or thoughts. I fairly chuckled at the idea; and perhaps he heard me; for he moved on the bed suddenly, as if startled. Now you may think that I drew back—but no.

His room was as black as pitch with the thick darkness (for the shutters were down from fear of burglars) and so I knew that he could not see the opening of the door and I kept pushing it on steadily, steadily. I had my head in and was about to turn on the flashlight, when my thumb slipped upon the button and the old man sprang up in bed, crying out, "Who's there? Sandski? Is that you?" I kept quite still and said nothing. For a whole hour, I did not move a muscle and in the meantime I did not hear him lie down. He was still sitting up in the bed listening—just as I have done, night after night, listening to the death watches in the wall.

Presently, I heard a slight groan and I knew it was the groan of mortal terror. It was not a groan of pain or of grief—oh, no!—it was the low stifled sound that arises from the bottom of the soul when overcharged with awe. I knew the sound well. Many a night, just at midnight, when everyone else slept, it has welled up from my own bosom, deepening, with its dreadful echo, the terrors that distracted me. I say I knew it well.

I knew what the old man felt and pitied him, although, I chuckled inside. I knew that he had been lying awake ever since the first slight noise, when he had turned in the bed. His fears had been, ever since, growing upon him. He had been trying to fancy them causeless but could not.

He had been saying to himself, "It is nothing but the wind in the chimney; it is only a mouse crossing the floor," or, "It is merely a cricket which has made a single chirp." Yes, he had been trying to comfort himself with these suppositions: but he had found all in vain.

All in vain; because Death, in approaching him, had stalked with his black shadow in front of him and enveloped the victim. And it was the mournful influence of the unperceived shadow that caused him to feel—although he neither saw nor heard—to feel the presence of my head within the room.

When I had waited a long time, very patiently, without hearing him lie down, I resolved to turn on the flashlight. So I pressed the button—you cannot imagine how stealthily, stealthily—until, at length a *simple dim ray, like the thread of the spider, shot from out the device and fell full upon the vulture eye. It was open—wide, wide open—and I grew furious as I gazed upon it. I saw it with perfect distinctness—all a dull blue, with a hideous veil over it that chilled the very marrow in my bones.*

But I could see nothing else of the old man's face or person. For I had directed the ray as if by instinct, precisely upon the damned spot. And have I not told you that what you mistake for madness is but over-acuteness of the sense?—now, I say, there came to my ears a low, dull, quick sound, such as a watch makes when enveloped in cotton. I knew that sound well, too. It was the beating of the old man's heart. It increased my fury, as the beating of a drum stimulates the soldier into courage.

But, even yet, I refrained and kept still. I scarcely breathed. I held the flashlight motionless. I tried to see how steadily I could maintain the ray upon the eye. Meantime, the hellish tattoo of the heart increased. It grew quicker and quicker and louder and louder every instant. The old man's terror must have been extreme! It grew louder, I say, louder every moment!—do you hear me! well, I have told you that I am nervous—so I am.

And then, at the dead hour of the night, amid the dreadful silence of that old house, so strange a noise as this excited me to uncontrollable terror. Yet, for some minutes longer I refrained and stood still. But the beating grew louder, louder! I thought the heart must burst.

And then a new anxiety seized me—the sound would be heard by a neighbor!

The old man's hour had come!

With a loud yell, I brandished the flashlight and

leaped into the room. He shrieked once—once only. In an instant, I dragged him to the floor and pulled the heavy bed over him.

"No one must find out I showered with those boys. I was just horsing around. I loved them. Therefore, the sex is fine," I said.

I then smiled gaily to find the deed so far done. But, for many minutes, the heart beat on with a muffled sound. This, however, did not annoy me; it would not be heard through the wall. At length it ceased. The old man was dead. I removed the bed and examined the corpse.

Yes, he was stone, stone dead. I placed my hand upon his heart and held it there many minutes. There was no pulsation. He was stone dead. His eye would trouble me no more.

If still you think me mad, you will think so no longer when I describe the wise precautions I took for the concealment of the body. The night waned, and I worked hastily but in silence. First of all, I dismembered the body. I cut off the head and the arms and the legs. I then took up three planks from the floor and deposited all between the scantlings. I then replaced the boards so cleverly, so cunningly, that no human eye—not even his—could have detected anything wrong. There was nothing to wash out—no stain of any kind—no bloodstain or whatever. I had been too wary for that. A tub had caught all— ha! ha! When I had made an end of these labors, it was four o'clock—still dark as midnight.

As the clock chime sounded the hour, there came a knocking at the street door. I went down to open it with a light heart—for what had I now to fear? There entered three men. Two introduced themselves, with perfect suavity, as officers of the police. The third one

I recognized instantly as that reporter from the New York Roast, Bryan Vacation.

A shriek had been heard by a neighbor during the night; suspicion of foul play had been aroused; information had been lodged at the police office and they (the officers) had been dispatched to search the premises. I smiled—for what had I to fear? I bade the gentlemen welcome. The shriek, I said, was my own in a dream. The old man, I mentioned, was absent—in the country—some sort of football camp or preseason practice. "I don't know for sure," I said.

I took my visitors all over the house. I bade them search—search well. I led them, at length, to his chamber. I showed them his treasures; secure, undisturbed. In the enthusiasm of my confidence, I brought chairs into the room and desired them to rest from their fatigues, while I, myself, in the wild audacity of my perfect triumph, placed my own seat upon the very spot beneath which reposed his remains.

The officers were satisfied. My manner had convinced them. I was singularly at ease. But that reporter—that Mr. Vacation. He looked like he was suspicious. He kept probing and kept on probing. Asking me questions and hoping I would crack. Mr. Vacation seemed sleazy but he had no evil bone in his body that I could see. Not the type of man who would plan a murder.

They sat, and while I answered cheerily, they chatted of familiar things. But, before long, I felt myself getting pale and wished them to be gone. My head ached and I fancied a ringing in my ears; but still they sat and still chatted. The ringing became more distinct—It continued and became more distinct. I talked more freely to get rid of the feeling but it continued and gained definiteness—until, at length, I found that the noise was not within my ears. No doubt I now grew very pale—but I talked more fluently, and with a heightened voice. Yet the sound increased—and what could I do? It was a low, dull, quick sound— much such a sound as a watch makes when enveloped in cotton.

I gasped for breath—and yet the officers heard it not. I talked more quickly—more vehemently; but the noise steadily increased. I arose and argued about trifles, in a high key and with violent gesticulations; but the noise steadily increased.

Why would they not be gone?

I paced the floor to and fro with heavy strides, as if excited to fury by the observations of the men—but the noise steadily increased.

Oh God! what could I do? I foamed—I raved—I swore!

I swung the chair upon which I had been sitting, and grated it upon the boards, but the noise arose over all and continually increased.

It grew louder—louder—louder!

And still the men chatted pleasantly, and smiled. Was it possible they heard not? Almighty God!—no, no! They heard!—they suspected!—they knew!—they were making a mockery of my horror!—this I thought, and this I think.

But anything was better than this agony! Anything was more tolerable than this derision! I could bear those hypocritical smiles no longer! I felt that I must scream or die! and now—again!—hear it! louder! louder! louder! louder!

"Villains!" I shrieked, "Dissemble no more! I admit the deed!—tear up the planks! here, here!—It is the beating of his hideous heart!"

"And you will also find the photographs as well as passwords of Internet accounts with pictures of all the boys I had relationships with. But, I loved them! There was no abuse!"

Bryan finished reading the confession. Sandski had written from his cell in Rikers, recounting what happened. Bryan banged out a headline and introduction:

ITHACA UNIVERSITY-NICKNAMED PENN STATE-COACH UNRAVELED BY MAVERICK REPORTER AND MARKETER, BRYAN VACATION
Coach Kerry Sandski, an Assistant Football Coach at Penn State under Moe Raterno, the Head Coach, was charged with 52 counts of sexual assault on young boys, ages 7-13. The creep, Sandski, abused these children through his charity, The Second Kilometer. *Apparently, Raterno knew all about it but kept silent.*
New York City detectives produced a stunning confession. Excerpted below, you can buy the full copy at our website for only 99 cents using online retailer Blue Gammamazon's Easy Pay program.

Bryan was happy with the headline. But it brought back a rush of feelings from his past. Like the night he met Blondie. Bryan used to go walking near Grand Central, mostly on Lexington or Third Avenue. That's where he first met Blondie.

His eyes strayed to the silky, red checkered tie on the desk. Expensive. He had used it as a bookmark inside the Staples notebook of Sandski's confession, but it had been used for many more nefarious purposes. It held many poignant memories, like the lives held in a hangman's noose.

He used to drop the expensive, iconic tie near a pretty woman and, when she went to pick it up, he would expose himself. The night he met Blondie, though, was different; she picked up the tie and stole his heart. The scars of childhood abuse at the hands of Coach Sandski made victims do funny things. But, revenge was his. He had the notebook with the killer story.

Bryan got excited thinking about all of the fucking and sucking that lay ahead. He texted Blondie that he was running late on an assignment and would be at her condo near Grand Central an hour later than he had originally hoped. He closed his laptop and shut off the light, taking time beforehand to put on his tie. It completed him. His look. His brand. Bryan Vacation. An excellent brand. And you don't fuck with the brand.

Bryan stepped into the nondescript building in Harlem shortly after dusk. A priest in his white collar came and greeted him. Bryan slipped him two hundreds.

"The *Catholic Boys Charity* appreciates your generosity, Mr. Vacation," the priest said.

Bryan smiled and nodded. The priest led him to a classroom with boarded-up windows situated in the middle of a long hallway on the second floor. Room 266. There were five dusty desks scattered around inside and piles of books leaned against each other like rubble in a Syrian village after a US bombing of ISIS centers.

Pushed up against an old blackboard was a worn, red leather couch—a black blanket draped over one arm. Bryan took a load off. The cushion squished nicely beneath the seat of his expensive suit pants. The priest crossed the room and opened an inner door, accessing an adjacent classroom. Bryan heard indistinct mumbling and a chair squealing on its legs as the priest nodded his head and opened the door wider. Adam, a 10-year-old boy with ebony skin darker than night, crossed the threshold within the welcoming embrace of the open-armed priest.

"Adam needs help with his homework. And, of course, he wants you to teach him about life," the priest intoned reverently.

Bryan smiled and signaled for the boy to come sit on the couch next to him. He caressed the leather with slow, circular motions. Adam walked towards him, trembling slightly. The priest left through the door he still held open and let it swing shut behind him. Excitement coursed through Bryan like ink being freshly tattooed on empty canvas, filling pores and layers upon layers of skin in an artful display of masochism at its finest.

Adam stopped in front of him, too shy to sit down, yet, next to Bryan, a famous reporter.

"Hi, little boy. Adam, you are a cutie pie," Bryan chuckled. "Let's see if I can't teach you a little bit about Biology. Ready?" He placed his hand encouragingly on Adam's shoulder.

"But first, I've got a tattoo that I think you'll find absolutely fascinating. Want to see it?"

PART III

UP

"...There is a time for silence. A
time to let go and allow people
to hurl themselves into their
own destiny. And a time to
prepare to pick up the pieces
when it's all over."

Octavia Butler

Status

i

Nathalya Hitler's Status: **You are my pink bubble gum because you expand my whole world and we make each others' heads blow up, lolz**

Nathalya Hitler had written this on Margarita's ceiling on THE_SOCIAL_NETWORK (TSN) as a status update in the early days of their love, long before either of them had any idea of the roller coaster ride they would go on. That's why John Lennon sang so eloquently: "Life is what happens when you are busy making plans."

Nathalya found the sound of rain very soothing. When she laid on the bed of her shiny sixty-nine-story skyscraper (half a mile from the train station in Freiburg, Germany), she liked to hear the sound of the trains gliding on the wet, stainless steel railroad tracks as it rained. Those sounds really calmed Nathalya.

She lay in bed and played absently with her curly

blond hair, her ocean blue eyes seeing something other than her latest post to TSN. She had piquant blue eyes that didn't quite match. Something was slightly off. No one would figure out why. Or would they? The funny thing is, whenever guys tried to pick her up, they would shout out the clichéd line: "Your eyes are blue like the ocean."

At first, Nathalya laughed. Lately, she wanted to puke. So boring. And unoriginal. She would twirl her pear shaped hips and walk away, her curly blonde hair swaying on her hips like a breeze over Redondo Beach on a midsummer's night.

The sound of the train wheezing by was especially tranquil on Monday, Wednesday, and Friday nights. Those were the nights when her father, Gunther, would come back home from the coal mines (precisely at 6:06 PM) after arriving at the station at 5:45 PM. Even though Gunther was a big, stocky man with a bit of a beer belly, he managed to walk rapidly back to the apartment in 21 minutes flat. Occasionally, he would slip and arrive at the doorstep one minute late at 6:07 PM.

Gunther would rush into the kitchen and smile at Nathalya. Nathalya would see his slightly yellowing teeth, softly rotting at the core. Nathalya kept her teeth religiously white and clean, though she had started smoking at 16 (five years ago). *I hope I don't get yellow teeth like Daddy,* she often hoped. "Hallo, Daddy," she would greet him (her English was fluent with a slight German accent). Nathalya would smile. There was nothing pleasant or pretty about her smile.

"How is my little angel?" Gunther would ask.

Then, after the obligatory pleasantries (which Nathalya felt dragged on far too long...*Can we get started already???*) they would eventually get to the point.

Gunther would rip his little girl's clothes off and penetrate her again and again. At first, Nathalya used to resist—protest. She knew it was...messy. Eventually, though, she gave up. He was much stronger. And the pain from the beating if she made him wait for his orgasm was ferocious as she lay bleeding. But, just as the biggest lies we tell can be the ones we delude ourselves into believing, Nathalya was convinced everything was hunky dory, A-OK, and peachy. Peaches are good, except for the rotten ones from Australia.

How could it not be A-OK? She smelled Daddy's masculine musk combined with her feminine scent on her after they fucked (made love? What's love gotta do with it?). And they had their intimate moments after Gunther came—Nathalya would fingerpaint a heart shape with his semen on his stomach and write *unconditional love*. Gunther may have been 48, but he was a twink—as the kids said. Hot and full of cum. One time, Nathalya even posted the picture of the semen-heart on TSN, and labeled it as:

Nathalya Hitler's Status: **Milk spilled on Daddy's stomach. :-P**

And, after all, she *was* Daddy's little girl. Nathalya just laid back spread eagle and succumbed or, if he were entering from the rear, put her head between her arms. She didn't remember when she started ignoring him while he grunted on top of her. But, these days, she found her mind floating away. To thoughts of Margarita Hernandez. Her Maggie.

"Remember, Nathalya—just remove yourself. It's just your body. He can't control your mind. And, in a few days, you will be in Palo Alto. Hola, California sunshine! It will all be over." Maggie had told her how wrong it was. Gunther's abuse. Nathalya ignored that, too, so she didn't have to think about it too hard.

As a train exited the railway station, Nathalya heard the rhythmic sound of the hard steel dancing through the wet rain like butter through a hot pan.

In bed, if Gunther were with her, he would say, "Daddy is fucking his little girl."

Nathalya's mouth opened slightly as she recalled the power of those words. She moved her lips and made a soft sound, like the rain swooshing on the window.

"Fuck me, Daddy," Nathalya would automatically rejoinder. Almost as a reflex. Without conscious thought. Like breathing.

These days, Margarita and the life that lay ahead entered her mind. Sunny California. *Soon, very soon*, she often told herself. Nathalya would be brought back from California dreams by Gunther's voice. His voice would sound very calm, relaxed. He was always like that post-coital. The sex calmed him down. Nathalya felt like Gunther was always aggressive beforehand— after working all day in the coal mines and from the almost 3 hour commute. Nathalya felt bad. The rain consoled her as it drizzled. She could almost smell it. Her family always had a low status in German society. Her mother left the family when Nathalya was just sixteen. On that night of her sixteenth birthday, Gunther was quite giddy."Daddy's girl is sweet sixteen, eh! Look at that. All grown up now."

"Love my Daddy." Nathalya's voice had trailed off that night.

The wind mumbled. A train screeched outside. That night, she had remembered her 8th birthday—when it had all begun. Back then, it seemed like status was all that mattered in society. And people like her family, with low status, had all the bad things happen to them.

The rain exhaled. Gunther had looked at her that night with a certain expression. Nathalya traveled from age 8 to age sixteen when Gunther had asked that night, "Where is my coffee, little girl?" "Just give me a minute, Daddy," she had replied softly. *Spare me the bullshit. You force-fuck your daughter. I get no feelings for this crap*, she thought, as she remembered that whole episode.

"One second, Daddy," she had said. "I need to update my status on THE_SOCIAL_NETWORK.COM."

Gunther had grunted. Then, he had flipped on his black phone, put a hand down his pants and started masturbating to pictures of Nathalya when she was ten.

"Like mother, like daughter. A mini-whore." Gunther had laughed. Nathalya had then updated her status.

Nathalya Hitler's Status: **I want to say thank you to all the people who shaped me. –––To all the people who disappoint me. To all the people who left scars...and sorry for all the broken hearts from my lovers. But most of all...unconditional love to everyone.**

1.5 seconds later—5,872 miles away in sunny Palo Alto, California—Margarita had hit the LUV button on THE_SOCIAL_NETWORK.COM. That action had been precipitated by many previous TSN chats the two shared, along with countless status updates luved between them, too. And many, many more luvs were shared between them from that day on. Nathalya sighed and flipped onto her stomach into TV Watching Pose; Nathalya heard the rain stutter slightly then pick back up. She glanced at her TSN profile. Lazily, she luved Margarita's most current status update:

Margarita Hernandez's Status: **Ariba! The girls and I are dancin' all night long, tonight! Ariba!**

Everyone hit the LUV button on everything. So much so that the notion of LUV, much like the notion of friendship on THE_SOCIAL_NETWORK .COM, had been diluted.

But not for Nathalya and Margarita. They both believed in their true, unconditional love for each other. And, although they would eventually die, they believed their unconditional love would survive.

Like Nathalya, Margarita had long hair—almost to the edge of her supple rear end. The rear that drove boys crazy. The kind of rear that seemed like a perky Southwest Airlines flight attendant, always sticking out subtly and saying hello. One big difference between their long hair, though, was Nathalya's hair was curly blond whereas Margarita's was dark.

Margarita worked as a nanny in Palo Alto. The Nannyluv Agency placed nannies with "host" families. It was a good deal for both parties and they exploited each other. The families gave the agency $1,800 per month for 200 hours of work. So, the agency got paid $9 an hour and paid their nannies half that, giving them a total of $870.75, keeping the rest as profit. Paying the nannies about $4.50/hr.

The beauty of the system is that the exploited class —the nannies—didn't care. They got a free ticket to America, a great place to stay in a rich family's home, and parties.

Yes, the status was part and parcel of the job. Underneath the veneer of, "We are all equal" (in Palo Alto) lurked the monster with yellow teeth and bad skin. Status *did* matter.

Status, as in—how much money did you make from THE_SOCIAL_NETWORK.COM's IPO? But, somehow, it felt *more* equal there. To the nannies and everyone else.

Gunther could never have dreamt of rubbing elbows with the same class of people Margarita did. And who Nathalya soon would, if a few key elements would fall into place. Although, Nathalya didn't quite understand what "rubbing elbows" entailed. Margarita told her that she would explain it in detail when Nathalya arrived in Palo Alto.

The parties. Ah, yes, the parties. Nathalya couldn't wait to get there for those parties. Margarita had told her all about the parties. And Nathalya had seen all of Maggie's posts on TSN. Photos with beautiful women partying with gorgeous guys. All night long. But Nathalya did not know a key piece of information. Margarita would tell her when she got there.

Nathalya was reaching her limit with the unorthodox relationship and forced sex with Gunther. So she had asked Maggie to help her. To help her get out. As Nathalya waited for Gunther's train to come in, she picked up her phone and pressed speed dial 2.

"Hola, Nathalya," Margarita sang down the line, her voice warm and honey coated. Like a lover's voice.

Her voice seemed so close to Nathalya. As her Maggie spoke, Nathalya heard a noise in the background. "What's that?" Nathalya queried.

"It's just Caltrain." Maggie said.

"Oh, cool motherchucker. Ha ha," Nathalya laughed. She liked the word motherchucker. Much softer than motherfucker. Drenched in love.

"So, ya, frauline, my host family lives just a few houses down from Steve Jobs. And I can hear the Caltrain pulling into the station behind Alma," Maggie said.

"I know, Maggie. Babe, it sounds like paradise. Soon we will be there together! Ariba, Ariba," said Nathalya. To her, everything was a party. America itself was the promise of one giant party.

"Listen, Nathalya, babe, did you get my gift?" Maggie asked.

"Not yet, honey. I will check in the lobby tomorrow morning."

The nanny crowd in the San Francisco Bay Area is very egalitarian. All the nannies are equal. But, some are *more* equal than others. Especially ones like Margarita, because of the whispers that she is an heiress to the Mexican Hernandez family. The Hernandez family is one of the major drug mafias; a Mexican Soprano, if you will. Margarita's Dad is the Tony Soprano/James Gandolfini of the crew.

It didn't take long for Nathalya to realize that Margarita could help her. In tangible ways. When she found the gift downstairs the next day in the form of a green Fedex package, her whole being radiated joy, though only her face beamed.

She sprinted upstairs. Nothing like a good sprint. *Feel the burn in your legs. Run, baby, run.* Lungs gasping for air, she started humming a song. A simple song of freedom. Just a few short steps away from sunny California.

As she re-entered the apartment, her euphoric state died as she saw Gunther frowning at her. He was wearing a red bathrobe and a stony expression.

"Little girl, what's that package?" Gunther attacked.

Then he farted and it sounded like a noise a stalled train makes.

"Oh, Daddy, it's nothing. I mean, just a little gift from my Maggie in California," she appeased.

"I don't find that very amusing."

Gunther wiped the sweat trickling down his brow. Blood rushed to his face and he seemed angrier by every passing second.

"Come, Daddy, we will make it amusing. Hey, Daddy, let's go have a beer!"

"Why? What are you hiding from me?"

"Nothing, Daddy. Love my Daddy, lots."

Nathalya edged closer to Gunther. She started rubbing her hands on his legs suggestively. She held her breath, disguised her desperation, and tried to remain calm.

Keep calm and eat bacon, Margarita had told her that one time.

That expression had made her laugh. Almost giggle. But as she rubbed his growing erection, she just breathed and prayed that she could get his mind off of her package. She resolved not to let Gunther find out at any cost that she would be running off to America.

Nathalya told herself that she was looking forward to her dinner with Gunther—Daddy dearest—happening later that night. If she could keep his mind off of her package by rubbing him until he orgasmed, she thought she could pull it off.

Before Gunther worked in the coal mines, he completed his PHD in mining sciences at the Freiburg Polytechnic Institute. In Germany—unlike in Palo Alto (where money is King, Queen, Prince, Princess, and The Pope, all wrapped up in a fluffy pink bow with glittery wrapping paper made of worthless stock options of start ups that aspired to be THE_SOCIAL_NETWORK (TSN) but never made it) a good education gave Gunther a certain amount of real prestige and corresponding status in society.

Gunther was a rebel and wanted to give society his big, hairy, middle-finger. The same claw he used to pleasure Nathalya, which she felt with a mixture of passion and horror, sprinkled with righteous anger like walnuts on a vanilla ice cream sundae. Hence, he chose to work a menial labor (not management) job in the coal mine—just like he chugged his pale ale lager beer when he stood in the drug line.

Nonetheless, Nathalya enjoyed the status that came with the good table at the restaurant, the backslaps from Daddy's intellectual University friends and the friendly banter that even curt and direct German waitresses made with Gunther because he was once quite the intellectual legend in his PHD days.

But, time fades and kills all and just leaves us with nothing, except boring stories and stale memories. Statistically, things remembered often subvert remembered things.

That was then. The memories, they faded. It was just a nice, upcoming dinner date, Nathalya told herself. Followed by a not-so-nice, I don't really wanna consent, can't wait til Margarita saves me, fucking-her-Daddy-sex. Just sex. Nothing more, nothing less, and absolutely nothing equal.

Nathalya stood near the doorway of the apartment with her *Daddy please hurry the fuck up, let's go to dinner* look on her face when the phone rang. Mommy dearest was on the line. Nathalya's mother sounded like she was out of breath after a 45-minute, 145 euro, bondage fucking session with a John. Or, in this case, a Borris.

"Hi, sweetheart," her Mom said.

"Mom, you told me there is an end. One more time: did YOU really believe this lie?" Nathalya fairly screamed.

Before her mother could answer, Gunther snatched the phone from Nathalya's hands like a cat grabbing a hummingbird at a backyard rose garden. Gunther's face was ruddy and his veins were pulsing like incoming messages over THE_SOCIAL_NETWORK (TSN).

"You leave my little girl alone, you crazy-cunt-whore! YOU are bad for Nathalya," Gunther spat. End Call.

Just as he had turned up the heat, in an instant—maybe 1/10 of a second—Gunther cooled down as quickly as one can change the TV channel or like a deflated mob on TSN, internet connections lost.

"Come, my little girl, let's go have dinner." Gunther's voice was soothing on top—romantic arousal—blended with menacing undertones.

Nathalya sobbed and held out her hands with pink, pianist fingers. She didn't notice the erection riding it's way down Gunther's jeans, the thick material keeping it under wraps.

"Daddy. I want to, uh, say thank you for having shaped me."

Nathalya smiled through her tears and it was oddly warm and genuine.

Maybe, after you tell a lie often enough, you internalize it as the true gospel. Deep inside of her, Nathalya was surprised by a morsel of little-girl-and-Daddy innocence. Popcorn love. Just like she had felt so long ago. Nathalya felt that it was a time very long ago, when dinosaurs roamed the earth. Long before Gunther started shoving his cock deep inside her mouth. Those days came and went like a fleeting romantic melody.

But soon—in 12.2 hours—her flight would take her to America and to freedom. Neugeboren (the German word for newborn) danced in her head, like visions of Margarita dearest.

Nathalya's favorite song was "Fall For Your Type," by Drake. The rapper. She didn't care that Drake's status in the rap community was a solid B, according to the Palo Alto Journal—after they (and their parent company THE_SOCIAL_NETWORK) bought the struggling NY Times Company for a mere $222 thousand dollars and free coffee for the 20 Manhattan based reporters they did not fire. Nathalya liked Drake. Thank you very much, come again, and now fuck off (or bugger off as the British nannies would say). The song "Fall For Your Type" reminded her so much of Margarita—her majestic Maggie, current reigning queen of the nanny gang.

But, could it also remind her of Gunther? Maybe? She shivered. Gross. Repulsive. *But I love my Daddy. Little girl wants Daddy's cock up her ass—and, sometimes, a sweet kiss for little girl from Daddy. Gently, softly on her pink cheeks while he slowly twirls his hairy fingers through her golden tresses...Little girl and Daddy. Together. Forever. In eternity...Little girl, Nathalya...*

She snapped back into awareness and found herself sitting at the dinner table. The table was empty because the waitress had shimmied away a few seconds prior and swept away the dirty dishes. Just little girl and Daddy, alone again.

"The morning will come and the world will be yours, little girl. Tomorrow belongs to *us*," Gunther was saying. Nathalya wondered how much of his monologue she had missed. His voice grated with dirt and his dirty fingers glided over her inner thighs like a seagull on the water on Half Moon Bay (approximately 26.2 miles from Palo Alto, straight as the black crow flies).

Nathalya felt a smile strolling to the corner of her mouth. "Daddy, we have so lived for the moment uninhibited. Our passion couldn't be tamed." She matched his fingers on her inner thighs. Their fingers interlocked. "The time we have had has been so intense, without rules and with deep feeling," she continued. She sighed and thought, *It was never a normal relationship, but it was OK, 'cause she already knew similar shit and Daddy did protect her from the harsh, outside world.*

Her eyes lit up. "Daddy, when I look at you, I smile all the time. Just for you. Even if I smile on someone else. I want you to see me happy," Nathalya stroked his ego as she stroked his thigh.

But it will never fucking happen. "Every dress I buy, I'm thinking if you would like it, because when I dance Daddy, I dance just for you," she said (her English grammar deteriorated as she imagined her future without Gunther in her life). *But your eyes, those goddamn eyes, will be following me everywhere. I will be burdened with thoughts of you all the time, even long after the last moment we share is already over...*

Daddy loves you. He told you that in some African tribes, the fathers have sex with their daughters. Totally natural. The fathers have status and can teach the virgin daughters how men should treat them. You are wrong Nathalya, he loves you. How about all the times you cuddle in bed and fingerpaint with Daddy's semen on his stomach...tender moments. No, not

tender. Sick. *But, who says that, Nathalya? Society.
Fuck society. Do you care about status....?*

"Little girl, I need to go to the bathroom," Gunther
interrupted her thoughts. His voice brought Nathalya
back from the whirlpool of conflict permeating her
brain and swimming in her heart.

"You go, Daddy. I am going to quickly talk to
Maggie on THE_SOCIAL_NETWORK. And I will get you
one more shot—one for the road," she cooed.

She giggled. Gunther airbrushed her hips and
lumbered to the bathroom.

Nathalya stood up and pushed the button on the
Instatalk feature on THE_SOCIAL_NETWORK. She
motioned for the bartender to fill Daddy dearest's
deadly drink (alcohol and smoking will kill you,
Gunther used to joke). She messaged Maggie over
TSN's messaging service: "It's time," she typed. She
then posted a status on THE_SOCIAL_NETWORK:

Nathalya Hitler's Status: **Enjoying farewell
Daddy dinner. Get ready, bitches in America,
here I come!**

Gunther came back from the bathroom and downed
his last drink. Nathalya and Gunther started walking
out of the restaurant and into the night. Fear flooded
her system like Route 280 floods on a rainy Palo Alto
evening.

I have no plan. I have no fucking plan! They were
only a few hundred feet away from the railroad tracks
opposite their apartment building. The silver bullet
train from Munich whistled as it approached the
station like an accelerating anaconda.

Gunther moved closer to Nathalya. Soon, he hoped
to be inside her. Nice, warm, and cuddly Daddylove.

He basked in the afterglow of the dinner and dreamt of the lengthy fucking and sucking session that stood in the doorway, waiting.

Nathalya's mind raced. *Tick, tock, clock is ticking. I have no plan?*

Nathalya tried very hard to push her nagging thoughts away. Too fucking late to plan because here was the train and when the headlights beamed towards them, she saw a momentary glimpse of Daddy's eyes. She also saw him wince against the red light, as she had, and knew that he was blinded. For only a split second. It was now or never. Nathalya thought, *I have no plan but tons of courage.*

Then (just as Margarita had predicted over many chat sessions on TSN) the colorless, odorless liquid that Nathalya had put in Gunther's drink took effect (the same one Margarita's cartel family used when they did not want another beheading in a Mexican border town to be shown on CNN). Gunther's heart was about to stop. It would look normal, just like a heart attack. The train roared closer and Gunther stumbled over the level crossing, directly into the path of the 169 mph locomotive.

Nathalya knew she loved Daddy, but sometimes...death is the best solution. She gave a little shove and that's all it took. The train hit Gunther on his head and his head flew and so did his entire body. The momentum ejaculated Gunther a few hundred yards away and his back lodged into a metal hook. His arms stuck up. He was a referee, signaling that the field goal was good.

Nathalya started to cry. It was mostly relief tinged with guilt. She pulled out her smart phone and posted a status on TSN:

Nathalya Hitler's Status: **Help! Daddy is in bad shape**.

She convinced herself of the lie. It would give her an alibi. And, sure enough, the German police were incompetent (not a thing like those in the last Philip Seymour Hoffman film). The interrogation was quick; the death was ruled an accident. "Such a shame," the Police Chief said. Because, at one time, Gunther had had education and the status and prestige that accompanied it like sauerkraut next to a hot dog. And...Bingo! Nathalya was in a Guber car (the super car service) on her way to the airport.

ii

Nathalya had just recovered from a 26 hour, Munich to San Francisco International flight (SFO as the natives in 2013 California called it)—2 stops in Amsterdam AND London (so the Nannyluv Agency could save fifty dollars) when she received an unexpected shock.

Margarita was much different in reality than the person Nathalya had thought she knew through the hundreds, if not thousands, of chats, messages, insta-talks and status updates on THE_SOCIAL_NETWORK; in 2013, in the San Francisco Bay Area...that was usually the case.

The Bay Area natives (and savages alike) often spent 30-40 hours a week on THE_SOCIAL_ NETWORK.

They carefully and meticulously built their "personal brand", leaving no detail to chance or spontaneity. In every party picture, Margarita and the nannies made sure they were with the right friends at the right Atherton houses with the right statuses. The poses had to be flawless and the smiles staged properly.

Conformity was of supreme importance to Margarita and her nanny friends. The group needed to be seen in the right light, with the right guys, in the right cars —Beemers, Mercedes, Porsches, and Testiclas.

They sneered at a girl who was dating an Indian guy with a few million net worth (not liquid, but who is liquid in tech?) who drove a mere $25,000 Subaru. "He is only worth $3.3 million and only 10% of that is liquid! Jaja!" Margarita said one time, as Nathalya contemplated the depth of her hatred for Maggie. Fake Maggie. Unreal Maggie. Maggie motherfucker! "No, thank you," Margarita had continued, as she thought of her family in Cancun, not knowing the dark thoughts and hatred boiling underneath Nathalya's picture-perfect, baby blue eyed, smiling mask.

Margarita then made a semi-circular motion with her hands (a similar motion to one that her family would make when they were chopping off the head of one of the $2/day workers in their cocaine manufacturing plant on the outskirts of the airport on the way to the $400/night hotel resorts where the $2 million trust fund babies from Palo Alto partied the night away while drinking $16 margaritas and chasing after $150/hour Mexican hookers) and Nathalya imagined a large knife slicing off Margarita's head. Thwack. Headless in seconds.

There was no shortage of guys chasing the 19 to 25-year-old nannies in Palo Alto. The pursuit of sex was a competitive bloodsport in Silicon Valley. Just like the technology industry. The nannies would gladly go out to $300 dinners at the restaurants that lined Sand Hill Road or Upper Broadway in Pacific Heights, San Francisco. They would go on their 36 hour trips to Vegas and party it up at Mandalay Bay or MGM Grand. All the while, their secret was safe.

The young Turks who pursued the nannies did get lucky on occasion. But only after they spent $1,000 on a girl. That was an unwritten rule that no one dared to disobey. Margarita made sure of that.

"Girl, don't spread your legs for nothing. Or for a $30 meal at the Hummus diner on University Avenue," Margarita ordered Nathalya, as she described what was in store for Nathalya now that the Nannyluv Agency had sponsored her ticket to the USA.

"Make them pay," Margarita ordered again and floated her arms in an up and down motion as her eyes met Nathalya's. Nathalya's shock was paramount. From Gunther to glorified prostitution in 26 hours. What had she gotten herself into? *Oh, well. Better saddle up, for now. Adapt or die.*

While all the nannies were equal, some were *more* equal than others. Nathalya felt that the white nannies subtly had more status or they *should* (*fuck this egalitarian, gorgeous mosaic, multi-cultural, American, CRAP, I am proud of Germany's Nazi past, and white people* are *superior. And now, mind you, we are more evolved, Neo-Nazi—we don't go around killing Jews*). And thank God for that because the Nouveau-Money in Palo Alto is 60% Indian or Chinese and only 40% White. Such is the way of Silicon Valley.

The open secret that the nannies knew but few outside their clique knew was that the Daddies (the fathers of the children they nannied) got the best and the most regular sex.

iii

Sometimes, Nathalya wrote meaningless songs and posted them to TSN:

Nathalya Hitler's Status: **Your infinite summer, you can see it fading fast. There is love all around, but, babyluv, you are driving too fast.**

She shared all of her poems with the nannies via TSN. She had to. Otherwise, she knew she would go mad. Gunther was bad enough. But the Nannyluv Agency had her in their grip. And the other nannies didn't care. They ate this life up with a spoon. The other nannies also ate up her poems and gushed, "Ooh, you are so talented and creative!!"

But her verses were only flashes in the pan. Like most people, Nathalya did not realize that creative says easy but does hard. Creativity sounds easy on the ears but it translates into long, hard hours staring at blank screens. Nonetheless, the adulation, social proof and the conformity she attained through sharing her verses were valuable currencies. Status was everything.

Dolores Park was like a large overgrown organic (fake, just for PR purposes) garden full of hippies, hipsters, nannies and sex chasers all mixed in the middle of the 60-90 degree hills that slope away on all sides to greet San Francisco abruptly. 'Sup bitches!

The park spent its wild days and mad existence (hail, Evita!) distributed between two elevations: A top rectangular area (decorated with beer cans, wine bottles, the last ⅛ inch of joints (medical marijuana, but of course), completed with used condoms) and a bottom grassy area (decorated with more of the same, sprinkled with doggy chocolate droppings on a green grass cake).

On San Francisco Gay Pride day, during a late afternoon when summer waltzed off stage towards autumn, Dolores Park was also full of flowers and flower children. It made Nathalya feel good to imagine Paul McCartney singing some romantic, joyful melody in her ear while she stood in the park.

Nathalya had been assigned as a nanny for Elvid, his wife Harmony and their autistic 6-year-old boy. Harmony put on her Hillary mask from 10-6 and did PR & Marketing for THE_SOCIAL_NETWORK. She convinced people that TSN wasn't evil and that they never sold data about their users (yeah, right). Her job paid for the $2.2 million renovation on their 2,200 square feet, Palo Alto home in Bryant Court. Their house was right around the corner from the 2nd Baptist Church and Steve Jobs's house. Their 'hood was very competitive about who could shell out the most money to the local construction firms for far-out and "socially conscious" renovations. No one could precisely define what the vague phrase "socially conscious" meant, however.

Perhaps the Chinese and Indian owners of the local construction firms were happy because they got tons of money and got to pay $12-13 an hour (under the table) to illegal Mexican aliens. They picked them up from the station at Chavez supermarket and taqueria on the Menlo Park-Atherton border, just a few miles up north. The dollars flowed and everyone was happy playing their part in the capitalist dance.

The California Avenue Caltrain station was walking distance from Elvid's house. Elvid told Nathalya (on her first day) a story about Steve Jobs. When Steve was alive, Elvid would lay out on the couch, late at night, and imagine how he and Steve Jobs (just 13 houses down) could hear the same whistle heralding an approaching train. A shared experience uniting everyone in the egalitarian silicon valley society. Although, some people were more equal than others because they had higher status.

Elvid introduced Nathalya to the 19.9 year old prodigy (the founder of TSN) on her second day at his house. The dude was a smart, blunt, tough guy from New York and Nathalya shook his hand outside of Antonio's Nut House. She melted. Later that same day, she didn't care that Elvid was 48 (more than 27 years her senior) (his wife, Harmony, was only 29.9 and much closer to Nathalya's age than to her husband's, as well). He had introduced her to an amazing guy. Nathalya let Elvid fuck her multiple times in his car that day while parked near the Quad on Stanford University's campus.

While his wife slaved away at TSN offices, Elvid putzed around the house. He "worked" on his novel. His novel would eventually be published when he paid $122,345 to an indie publisher. This was the type of thing in polite, New York social circles that they called "vanity publishing".

Most days, after she became accustomed to life in Palo Alto, Nathalya would use rose scented body wash (which Harmony had bought for her from the Stanford Shopping Center Body Shop on the first of their female bonding trips, her third day in Palo Alto). Nathalya would shower and use the body wash early in the morning. She took long showers and made lazy bubbles on her skin with the decadent soap. She loved the feel of it as it slid over her skin.

After eating breakfast, Nathalya would school Elvid in the ways of babymaking while Harmony's little baby boy was tutored. Elvid needed to learn a lot about the fine German art of making babies. Or rather, in the process that leads up to procreation, without ever actually creating an implanted embryo. Nathalya knew a thing or two about the subject, having been schooled herself by Gunther.

Elvid told her that their sex sessions were no big deal to Harmony. Not even worth mentioning to her. Harmony understood.

"You see, Nathalya," he began on her first night at their house, "this activity helps us bond, reduces our stress levels and creates a loving atmosphere. This will help you acclimate to life here much quicker, I promise. And Harmony wants you to acclimate smoothly. She wants stability for our son."

He had then stuck his tongue down her throat and fingered her until she came all over his middle finger. Then he fucked her hard against the wall, his balls slapping her labia with each thrust. Nathalya knew he badly needed some lessons in fucking after that.

Nathalya also understood that if she didn't spread her legs, Elvid would send an email to the Nannyluv Agency, drive her to SFO for the next plane back and immediately start looking for a replacement nanny. Margarita had told her in no uncertain terms that saying no was not an option.

All of the agencies in the nanny business knew that sometimes things didn't work out and the chemistry or fit wasn't harmonious. These code words had the same implied association as sleeping together had to fucking. It was important to people to sugarcoat things to preserve their status.

Nathalya didn't feel like dealing with a farty detective who had just ingested fifty frankfurters and answer fifty-five questions about Daddy dearest's death, among other things she'd have to endure if she were sent back to Germany. So, she spread her legs and never said no to Elvid.

In Palo Alto, the nanny Daddies didn't care that their cash, power and San Francisco Bay Area location gave them more leverage in the negotiations. Sexual consent was a mere formality. Some people would argue that sex under coercion, or manipulation, is rape. Berkeley educated Elvid knew better; it was only persuasion. His status happened to afford him the best persuasive techniques. It would be un-American not to wield the power he could over the nannies he hired. Not to use his status to his advantage and gain free sex whenever and wherever.

You might be wondering how we learned all of this information. Don't think about it. Just read on.

Elvid told his TSN wife dearie that Dolores Park was a great place for the nannies to socialize with each other. He didn't tell her about the extended doggy style fucking sessions he enjoyed there with Margarita beside the abandoned railroad tracks that snaked their way into the park. Elvid and Nathalya had also done reverse cowgirl in his pickup truck while parked at

Point Lookout off 280, on the way up to San Francisco, before getting to the park.

Elvid played Drake's "Fall for your type" on the drive (Nathalya's favorite, go figure) and thought it was a neat subliminal touch that could help Nathalya appreciate him. To erase any remaining doubts, Elvid told Nathalya about these African tribes he'd heard about where it was customary for the fathers to have sex with their daughters. Nathalya stared forward and counted the mile markers as they passed.

Elvid had a grand time that afternoon, on Gay Pride day. He drank organic beers with the group of nannies who were there, smoked medical marijuana that they had gotten at Kaiser (free through their health plans) and indulged himself with shamefully staring at their nubile bodies as they hung out and danced with each other. Margarita took her top off and applied blue tape to her nipples (forming 2 X's). After a few drinks, Elvid thought they resembled those on the Swiss flag.

He watched with delight as the nannies shook their asses and kissed random guys, girls, and transgenders. Margarita then got Nathalya to shed her top and tape her nipples, too. Margarita swapped saliva with Nathalya, positioning her boobs to rub up against Nathalya's and cause their nipples to harden. Margarita tongued Nathalya, felt her up and down and cupped her breasts. Margarita found Nathalya's lips very attractive, her boobs beautiful and erotic. Nathalya had never been with a woman before and found the experience sensual and exotic.

Margarita slowly lifted Nathalya's skirt, plunging her hand into Nathalya's dampened panties. Soon, Margarita knelt in front of Nathalya (her knees cushioned in the soft earth of the park) and positioned herself between Nathalya's legs. She slowly drew

Nathalya's panties down, pulling them all the way to her ankles.

Elvid watched with dilated pupils as Margarita's head disappeared under Nathalya's skirt. Nathalya moaned and Elvid could see Margarita's breasts jiggling up and down as she tongued Nathalya's inner lips. Elvid's erection grew faster than a lightning bolt could strike, his own wetness dripping down his thigh as he watched Nathalya grasp Margarita's head and arch her back. Her legs shook, her body quaked and an orgasm ripped through her body like a piece of shrapnel. Margarita kept licking throughout Nathalya's orgasm and Elvid saw Nathalya catch a glimpse of what unconditional love was all about. Unconditional love was getting licked while orgasming. It was being bathed in love.

A few hours after orgasming, Nathalya stood with Margarita and watched her smoke. "Maggie," she said, "I can feel your regret forming while you smoke that cigarette." Inside, Nathalya thought: *Brown, Mexican, drug family cunt. Who are you to lick me down there? After everything else, you, too, face fucked me over.*

"It's okay, Nathalya darling," Maggie lied. She forced a smile out of the corners of her mouth as her eyes wandered over the San Francisco hills. "It's okay," she repeated. *Cunty, smelly, white German*, Margarita bitched inside.

Of course it wasn't okay. Elvid loved Nathalya more and that was never going to be OK. All of the nannies and their groupies had begun to love Nathalya more and Margarita was never going to be OK with that.

Margarita held out her phone and mouthed, "I love you, Nathalya," before posting:

Margarita   Hernandez's   Status: **Unconditional**

love, Nathalya!

Nathalya reciprocated and posted a selfie with her biggest smile on her face:

Nathalya Hitler's Status: **Unconditional love, Margarita! Love ya!**

Just afterward, a breeze from the Pacific Ocean (a few miles away from where Robin Williams hung himself) flew in and changed the warm, sunshiny, good day feeling into a colder, foreboding microclimate, dark cloud feeling.

A fight sprang up between the two lovers. Elvid didn't hear all of it. He caught the ending.

Nathalya shouted: "You just blame everybody else. Can't you see it? Nobody cares. It's your fucking screwed-up life Margarita. So start blaming yourself!"

The unconditional, hippie, free love veneer had melted away from the scene. Like melted wax revealing a hidden prize inside the candle. Elvid could see that Nathalya was livid. She huffed and puffed and walked away from Margarita like the big bad wolf. Elvid was confused. Why couldn't they just eat each other out again and make up? His head pounded as the drugs he'd ingested made their presence known.

The other nannies noticed the blood pulsing underneath the surface of Nathalya's pale, white skin as she marched toward them, leaving Margarita alone. Elvid followed her, anxious to understand what had just happened. Margarita stood still where Nathalya had left her. Margarita saw the distance growing between them and her heart sank. She realized the significance of what Nathalya was doing and what it meant. Nathalya had made it clear. Margarita was an outsider. Her world turned dark, as if the moon covered the sun.

Nathalya reached the group. Inside, she was certain that she had to do something more to end Margarita's reign as the nanny queen. Margarita had to be held accountable for her lies and her false promises. Nathalya's problems would be over? Margarita had lured her into an even more dangerous viper nest, with more Daddies than she could count. An endless amount of Daddies who would use and abuse her. Just like Gunther. Just like Elvid. And those African fathers, whoever they were.

Nathalya hid her inner musings from her peers. She showed them a face that she usually kept in a jar on the nightstand (next to the various lubes and red condoms she and Elvid gobbled up during their fucking and sucking sessions). A party face.

"Ariba, bitches! Let's party!" Nathalya enthused. Elvid felt better immediately. This was more like it. Party time, not drama time.

Margarita drifted back unnoticed and stood on the outskirts of the group. The other nannies were focused on Nathalya, who was giving Elvid a risqué lap dance as he sat on an upturned crate. Elvid had a smile on his face like the cat that has the cream and the mouse.

Margarita took out her phone.

Margarita Hernandez's Status: **Party!**

But she wasn't really partying.

Back in the old days of 2013, by the University Avenue Caltrain stop in Palo Alto (instead of a 3D printing shop and 24 hour Subway Sandwich Shoppe) stood Rudy's bar. The exterior of the bar was red brick. Nondescript. Similar to hundreds of other California buildings. The floor was a mixture of sawdust, sand, peanut shells and condoms floating atop a dried mixture of beer, vodka, wine and bodily fluids. The condoms were the most visible. A cornucopia of used condoms, colorful and flavored like bananas, limes, or coconuts.

The sand on the floor was tracked in by the myriad patrons. The nannies brought in sand from Carmel. The nannies frequently had their boys take them to Carmel by the Sea for the art galleries. To catch a glimpse of former mayor Clint Eastwood. And to fuck and suck at the quaint bed and breakfasts, complete with lavender sachets, art deco paintings (straight from Miami) and cute tabby cats in the lounges.

The windows in Rudy's were tinted and neon lights waltzed around the stage as the Karaoke flowed as freely as bittersweet beer on a Wednesday night. On any random night, 30 to 40 nannies would be on the dance floor with 60 guys trying to catch their attention. Vying for the prettiest ones. They were like the mafia of silicon valley (not the much better known Indian mafia composed of a bunch of tech geeks who made it big). They were the nanny groupie mafia.

They all would stand or dance in a circle, each holding their drinks with only four fingers. Everyone would glance sideways at everyone else to ensure they had the right pose. They needed the right pose for casually hanging out in order to post authentic pictures of themselves on TSN. Conformity was rewarded in 2013 by more unconditional love on TSN from the horde.

Rudy's bar was just the right place to be for that. It was right next to the Caltrain University Avenue station. Quite convenient for drunk nannies hopping on the train totally smashed when they could not manipulate, sweet talk or blowjob their way home. If they were successful, the tech guys would shell out for a super duper Uber (no one used Lyft) ride back to San Francisco for them. Free rides for the nannies. Well, at least, no money ($269 surge pricing) was taken. Just the lost integrity of one or two of their holes. No biggie.

On the night in question, the vibe was different. Nathalya walked into Rudy's that night as the unofficial new Queen Bee of the nannies. She could smell the cheap perfume that they were wearing. It barely masked the scent of their dripping inner lips, sexed up earlier in the day by the Daddies.

Nathalya walked past the bar to the karaoke area and the dance floor. Right away, she noticed things were different that night.

Or maybe it was just a delusion?

The pack of nannies and their sausages seemed less tight physically. The circle was no longer one, 8 person diameter, symmetric, perfectly formed circle. It was several disjointed looser circles. People seemed unsure where to stand. How to hold their drink. How to pose the right way for the best TSN status updates.

Nathalya had dethroned Margarita in Dolores Park. Margarita was no longer at the center of the group. The nannies knew there was a new sheriff in town. She was German and blonde. There would be no more unconditional love for Margarita; a dirty whore; the daughter of an uncivilized Mexican drug cartel.

The happily married head of Stanford's medical school (a 59-year-old doctor) whispered to his 20-year-old undergraduate, blonde, model wannabee, student. Nathalya heard the whispers as she passed, her gaze on Margarita.

"You should bring her in to see me," he whispered, his breath heavily cloaked in vodka. "My sister's only sixteen," his student pointed out. "Yes. Bring her in. She needs an exam," he said, a little louder. Wink, wink. Nudge, nudge.

"What kind of exam?" His blonde student slurred her words, her gaze and voice clouded with booze. "A medical exam, of course," her married boyfriend soothed. He convinced himself that this lie was the truth.

Nathalya visibly gagged. She angrily pushed past them, a pathetic, drunk Daddy getting ready to test drive a younger version of his girlfriend. Cheating on his wife continually with younger and younger girls. Nathalya reached Margarita and punched her 4 times on the shoulder, harder each time. She poured her frustration and disgust out onto Margarita, a snake who falsely wore savior skin on TSN. Luring Nathalya here to this pit.

Margarita turned. Pain shot through her neck and embarrassment flooded through her. The group looked away, pretending to dance or to see something interesting posted on TSN. They were conformists, but not stupid. Mostly. They knew that Natalya was about to school Margarita. To chew her ass out.

Heads would roll.

The nannies would deny that they knew what was coming, of course. Not because they lie or they are bad (who can judge another?) but they keep secrets from themselves and they are afraid. We are all afraid sometimes.

"I tried to save the world and to make the right decisions. I woke up and realized how I want to live my life. Because everything happened for a reason. As long as *you* are alive..." Nathalya began, her voice steely.

Margarita shook from head to toe. She could see the nannies turning on her. Many of them were giving her the evil eye and the middle finger. Nathalya had made her point in Dolores Park, had gained her power, but Margarita could see that she wasn't done yet. A voice whispered inside Margarita's head: *Kick them when they are down*. It was her father's voice. Spoken to some lackey at some point in the past. Margarita had not understood what it meant, at that time. With Nathalya posturing in front of her and the nannies backing her up, Margarita finally understood that saying.

"Now, I know how you work Margarita. And it's creepy. Now I know you can't be trusted. None of us can trust you. I get no sympathy for all this crap. Your drama. Your bullshit," Nathalya spat. Inside, she was trying not to cry. *Be strong*.

Nathalya raised her voice to be heard clearly above the din of the bar. Her icy blue eyes looked like they could pop out of her head.

"We are all working hard to live our dreams, but it's harder than it seems. I still don't get it. How you complain, Margarita, and don't want to change!" Nathalya wanted to lash out. All of the times she let Daddy inside her. How could he? How could he do that to her? She was too afraid to defy him but now she could scream and let out her bottled rage onto Margarita.

Margarita broke. Tears poured down her cheeks as freely as the beer at the bar and the karaoke from the sound system.

The entire group gave up on any pretenses that their phones were more exciting than this cat fight. They gave up the red, vanilla scented rouge of pretend. There was nothing better going on in TSN than what was unfolding directly in front of them. The showdown between Nathalya and Margarita was infinitely more important and unique than anything happening on their phones. A watershed moment. The Mexican head of the nanny gang was being dethroned by the blonde German girl with the fuck-me-now booty. This was blood being spilled in real life. Everyone secretly started to imagine how they could have their Andy Warhol, 15 minutes of fame. How could they use this to be drenched in status love? On TSN?

Margarita swallowed, unable to think of any reply to Nathalya's onslaught. That's often the case. When confronted with the truth, the brain can shut down. Margarita tried to detach herself from the moment, as she felt all of those eyes on her, every nanny relishing in her downfall. A vision from her past appeared before her eyes, a sunny summer solstice in Mexico City. She had helped her family behead a father, a son and their holy dog. They had tattled on the cartel to some crazy CNN reporter.

"*You don't fuck with the cartel,*" her father had said before beheading the dog. "*These are the rules,*" her mother said, as she beheaded the son. "*This is the world of you poor, unfortunate Mexicans who stand in our path,*" her uncle had rasped as he sliced off the head of that father kneeling before them, pathetic enough to think he could stand a chance against Margarita's family. Margarita got blood on her favorite shoes as she stood there, waiting to help position the bodies in an artful display. A display that would remain in the heads of any other poor Mexicans who dared tattle on her family.

Margarita snapped back to her own situation in Rudy's, Nathalya's arms raised triumphantly in front of her face. Margarita could see beads of sweat dancing down Nathalya's shaved underarms and could smell her rose body wash. Nathalya was mad. Really mad at her. That anger could lead to things worse than death. Sometimes, death is the better option. Margarita had nothing to say. Her mind was blank. The smell of roses had her hypnotized.

Margarita's salty tears tugged at Nathalya's heart. Nathalya rhymed, "Life is too short to waste your time with useless things. Find your sense and live like kings." *Mmm….I like the sound of that*, she thought. *That was pretty good improv*.

Margarita continued to cry. The rose scent in her nostrils brought back memories of Dolores Park, before Nathalya spurned her. The way that Nathalya's inner lips had tasted. Nathalya tasted so good. Her wetness tasted like Christmas morning to Margarita. She imagined tasting Nathalya on the Stanford Quad, steps away from the Stanford Startup Memorial church. To lay there and lick and taste Nathalya again and again as the mown grass tickled their skin. To relish in Nathalya's taste as the $15/hr illegal Mexican workers watched from a distance. It was a dream that began the moment she tasted Nathalya's wetness. But it died a *petite mort* a few short hours later. Margarita imagined bending down and tasting Nathalya right then and there. In the heat of her anger. Surrounded by all the nannies. Margarita longed to lick Nathalya and dissolve her anger. To melt it into love. Unconditional love.

"Come on Maggie, let's do a song," Nathalya said suddenly. She glanced from Margarita to the karaoke stage.

Margarita hesitated. She could almost taste Nathalya's wetness. She wanted to give Nathalya an orgasm, not stand on stage in front of strangers and sing. She heard her uncle's raspy voice in her head: "*Sometimes you need to let the power go, Maggie.*" A few minutes after that, Margarita's father had chopped her uncle's head off with a black Gin Soohong knife (her father had bought the knife while watching late night TV at the Hilton across from the border in San Diego).

Margarita convinced herself that things would be fine. She would sing and then give Nathalya an orgasm. Nathalya had unconditional love for her. It was all over TSN. It must be true. Their statuses containing their declaration of limitless and eternal love was even endorsed by their drag queen friends (who had recently won their battle with TSN to use their stage names rather than their real names).

Margarita headed to the stage and told herself that things were fine. Liar, liar pants on fire. Nathalya wrapped her arms around Margarita, their blonde and dark locks intertwined like two cute kittens napping together. The gang of nannies saw their fingers interlocked. They were wearing matching purple nailpolish, courtesy of the $90 manicures that Elvid gladly covered (who said sex was cheap?).

Nathalya's white skin and Margarita's brown skin joined together at their hands.

White supremacy from Germany will rule the nannies and heads will roll, Nathalya thought. Daddy dearest would be very proud. *Yeah, he would be! Why did you have to kill Gunther off, you crazy cunt? It's just sex! No big deal! Don't be American and make it into a tool of manipulation and deceit!* Nathalya's inner voice dueled itself.

Margarita skipped forward and hoisted her small frame onto the stage. Nathalya clasped her hand tightly. They both made sure that they posted a video status on TSN mouthing, "Unconditional love," in that moment.

Nathalya Hitler's Status: **Unconditional love, Maggie girl!**

Margarita Hernandez's Status: **Unconditional love, Nat!**

"Nathalya. Please, promise me. You will never let go," Margarita said. Her voice was calm on top, desperate on the bottom.

"I will never let go," Nathalya lied. The lie was so convincing that she believed it herself, because the most persuasive lies are the ones we tell ourselves in life.

They selected the song, "My Heart Will Not Sing Without You" for Margarita's karaoke song. The song was from a cheesy romance where this guy Jack and this girl Rosamund were in a boat in the middle of a lake with the Loch Ness monster. Only one of them could live. This song was sung by Rosamund during rolling credits.

"My heart weeps for you every day when I shave my creamy inner thighs..." The lyrics appeared on the screen and Margarita crooned.

The crowd watched, phones out. Video apps on. The nannies knew what was about to happen next. So did Nathalya and three of Rudy's employees. The rest were surprised.

The next set of words appeared on the screen: "Margarita is a dirty, Mexican, cunt, whore and her pussy smells like fish tacos".

This took Nathalya three five-minute blowjobs. One to the head bartender, one to the Samoan doorman and one to the Fijian security guard in the back room. Dirty deeds were done dirt cheap. In 2013, you could get anything if you were willing to pay the price for it.

Margarita was still smiling when she saw the words. She could sense that there was something wrong, but couldn't quite nail it down, beyond a vague unease. Nathalya, the ever efficient German, snapped a selfie of the ephemeral moment. From her angle by the stage steps, she captured the juxtaposition of Margarita smiling (but not realizing that the pack was laughing at her and not with her), Nathalia's revenge fueled afterglow face and the look of joy and bloodlust on the faces of the crowd. Some of them were delighted to see Margarita, "15 minutes ago, I was your fearless leader" fall. The photo became a work of art in THE_SOCIAL_NETWORK (TSN) D (domain).

Nathalya Hitler's Status: **Margarita's Karaoke Photo**

People's perceptions of the speed of time vary based on a myriad of situations in life. Margarita felt that time was moving too fast and she couldn't keep up. Nathalya's status update went viral. 0 to 300,000 luvs in a mere 30 seconds.

The crowd began to chant, "Go back to Mexico, you dirty whore!" Their glee and laughter sometimes interrupted their rhythm midstream. Bottles, limes and oranges from the bar were thrown. A shower of condoms followed, led by Nathalya's chant: "Better wear several condoms and pray that you don't pick up some Mexican gonorrhea from this cunt!" Nathalya had gotten status and she used it with impunity. *There is a new German Sheriff in town! Watch out, you brown skinned, Mexican whore! Maggie dearest! Hah!* All along, Nathalya convinced herself that this was the most potent expression of unconditional love.

Margarita began to cry again and quickly folded into a fetal position on the stage. No bouncers or security came because they were too busy fucking some of the nannies doggy style in the back, courtesy of their German babe-cum-sister, Nathalya.

Nathalya went up on the stage and made sure everyone could see her extending her hand (Singapore Airlines flight attendant smile on her face) to help her Maggie dearest off the stage. To make sure there was no risk, Nathalya made sure she snapped a selfie to post on TSN.

Nathalya Hitler's Status: **Helping Maggie Dearest off the stage**

Nathalya's mind bubbled with the final solution as she pulled Margarita close and whispered: "Margarita baby, you fucked with Nathalya. Fucked with me and face fucked me, you whore. But, I will give you a chance. Run now. Go to Churchill Avenue. Get there before the last train from San Francisco. Put your head down on the tracks. Kill yourself. Death is the best way." Margarita heard no emotion in Nathalya's voice, just grit.

It made sense to Margarita. She had to kill herself. That was the only honorable thing to do. Otherwise, who knew what Nathalya had in store for her? She couldn't fight Nathalya. She wanted to bury her face in Nathalya's lap too much for that. Killing herself was the only way forward. For herself, for her family back in Mexico, for Nathalya, and for the whole group. She could save face if she killed herself. She could show everyone that she conformed to group norms.

"Nathalya, promise me. You will post a good TSN status update if I kill myself? Tasting you was the highlight of my life," Margarita said.

Nathalya smiled. "Of course, Maggie. Unconditional love. Now, go babe. Find your paradise on the Caltrain tracks." Nathalya stroked Margarita's hair tenderly. She bent and kissed her, their tongues and warm saliva mixing together, their fingertips caressing each other's nipples. Nathalya snapped a selfie of their kiss.

Nathalya Hitler's Status: **Kissing my dear Maggie. Unconditional love**

They stepped offstage together. Margarita then left

Nathalya and walked quickly through the bar to greet the outside air with a renewed sense of purpose. She hadn't been able to stand being an outcast. She wouldn't have to endure that fate. *Only 1.2 miles from Rudy's to Churchill crossing*, she told herself. *Must meet my destiny. Thank you, Mother Mary, for bringing me Nathalya. For all this unconditional love, even in my death.*

Margarita then ran hard. The next-to-last Caltrain from San Francisco claimed her blood a few minutes later. But it ended up being only the first, certainly not the last, blood of the night.

V

Nathalya stopped at the doorstep of Elvid's two story house with a red roof shaped like cannolis. Elvid got out his keys. She could see the shadow of the Baptist church, at the end of Bryant Avenue, bird dogging the house like the men hovered over the nannies during Karaoke at Rudy's. She was trying very hard to maintain her mask of composure. Elvid, standing next to her, saw right through her. Once you let someone into your body, they can usually wander into your soul, as well.

"Little girl, Nathalya. What's wrong, sweetheart?" Elvid asked. *Strange, he sounds like Daddy*. In the post-midnight light, Nathalya thought she saw something off about Elvid. His eyes seemed red. Red like Daddy's bathrobe. It seemed as if there were something evil or diabolical lurking in their depths. *Tsk, tsk, tsk, it's just your imagination. It's Elvid. Your employer. Your friend, mentor and occasional fuck buddy*.

Although his modern house (the "I gutted the old house with my millions of stock option money from

THE_SOCIAL_NETWORK" so "I could be in the 'my dick is bigger' house" because "I can top your measly $2 million to $1.5 million in renovations" and "I live closer to the executives of TSN that matter" house) was next to the Baptist Church, Nathalya told herself there was none of that Jesus vs. Lucifer stuff here. Only unconditional love. Just like the kind she has (had?) with Margarita.

"Look Da, uh, Elvid. I will tell you about it in the morning. Rough night, gotta sleep babe," she wheedled.

"Can we just fuck for a bit? Or will you give me a quick blow job?" Elvid whined. He was horny like a 13-year-old boy. Boys never outgrew their primal urge to stick their dicks in something wet in 2013. Preferably between consenting hips, if possible. He opened the door and followed Nathalya to her room on the ground floor, perfectly positioned for late night coitus. Nathalya put her clutch on the nightstand, kicked off her heels and turned to see Elvid shedding his clothes at the edge of her bed. She was exhausted emotionally and physically, but she obliged with machine like efficiency. She blew him hard and then took him between her legs against the wall, his semen rocketing out of him and into her womb faster than ever before. He loved wall fucks better than anything else. It made him feel manly and strong that he could hold her up.

Nathalya wondered if, this time, the odds would be against them. If it were a time (the 1% chance kind of time) that her birth control would fail. Were they creating a tiny Elvid-Nathalya love child at that very moment? The idea kind of turned her on. Elvid was flaccid but still inside her. She wrapped her legs around his waist and whispered, "Carry me to the bed,

Elvid." It had a nice cadence to it, what she had said.

He obliged and slid out of her. She held her legs up as he got dressed, watching him through her opened thighs. She could feel his semen trying to trickle out, gravity pulling it towards her anus. She lifted her legs higher up and scooted back into her pillows. Elvid didn't ask her what she was doing; he was too busy buttoning up his shirt. She asked him to give her a tampon out of the box in her closet. He gave it to her and then left, closing the door behind him. Nathalya reached down and slipped the newly opened tampon inside of her. She felt dangerously giddy. Keeping Elvid's semen inside of her was ridiculously easy.

She finally put her legs down on the bed and relished in the knowledge that she could be assisting her reproductive system into creating a baby. The only real goal the brain transmits from generation to generation: Split gamete cells. Make one into two. She pulled the covers over her nakedness and glanced toward the window. She was more than slightly shocked to see Margarita out of the corner of her eye.

Margarita's body was covered in weeds, dirt, and gravel from the railroad track. Her head was clearly severed from her torso but it dangled on top of her neck as if held together with duct tape. "You are supposed to be dead," Nathalya stated. She noticed that she was having difficulty breathing. "Babe, every step I take towards you, you step one back. I don't know what else could I do. Tried talking to ya a 100 times but you won't let me finish my lines," Margarita rasped.

Nathalya noticed a difference in Margarita's voice; it sounded like she had smoked three packs a day for twenty years. "Maggie, let me explain," she pleaded.

"Your game is not fair, Nathalya. You let me suffer

from your behavior," Margarita broke in. "I am not dead until I am dead to you. As long as I am here with you, and you acknowledge my presence, I am alive," Margarita gushed.

Margarita smiled and Nathalya noticed that when she smiled, half her teeth were gone. Grass and a Caltrain paper ticket ($7.25, Zone 3 to Zone 1) were sticking out of Margarita's gaping mouth. "Stop gambling with the wrong cards, Margarita. You had your final chance," Nathalya blustered.

She grabbed her phone out of her purse on the nightstand and posted a new status on TSN:

Nathalya Hitler's Status: **So sad, just heard that my dear Margarita is dead :(**

She snapped a photo of Margarita standing in front of her and applied a filter to post it on TSN. As the status hit TSN, Margarita's body began to disintegrate. "No, Nathalya, how could you do it?" The thing that was Margarita gasped. Her body burst into flames. Whoosh! Margarita disappeared into dust. It had happened only after her Nathalya, her so-called "unconditional love", had acknowledged her demise on TSN.

Elvid heard the commotion from the kitchen as he was getting a drink of water and ran back into Nathalya's room.

vi

"Nathalya! What happened? What was that noise?" Elvid asked. Nathalya couldn't remain quiet anymore. She told Elvid the whole truth. Nothing but the truth. Alas, there was no God to help either of them. In life, they were on their own in 2013.

"NATHALYA!" Elvid's voice shook as he whisper-shouted her name so that Harmony and his son would remain asleep. "Your father raped you in Germany?"

Nathalya nodded. "My father. Daddy dearest. Unconditional love, that's what he used to tell me. He said the steak knife with the 10 inch blade he held at my neck was to train me in the art of Daddy love. I kept still, and motionless. I was scared. But, one day, after band camp, when he came, the knife slipped." Nathalya pulled down the lower lid of her left eye with her left hand. She cupped her right hand beneath the eye and her glass eye rolled neatly into it. Nathalya's eye socket was empty and red.

"I can't find the sense of all this. Bullshit, what he did to me. He never regretted all the scars he gave me. He just thought about himself. No room for different opinions. No room for myself," Nathalya said, her eye held loosely in her cupped hand. "All his slanders can't push me down anymore," Nathalya continued emphatically, her opinion of herself restored through the unconditional love she got from the horde on TSN.

Elvid nodded sympathetically, but deep down inside, he knew what he had to do. "I should give him thanks instead of blame," Nathalya said next, "'cause he made me into a fighter without shame." Nathalya looked up at Elvid. She thought she could post that next on TSN. It sounded pretty good.

"Nathalya, I am sorry," Elvid began. "But, I have to go to the police and turn you in."

Nathalya's world turned black. Like the moon covering the sun. Just as Margarita had thought about her own world, in Dolores Park. Nathalya shivered. First, Gunther's murder could be laid at her feet. And then, Margarita's bullying suicide. She was sure they would nail her. Jail. Worse yet, deportation to Germany. And she would lose face with the nannies. They could not see their new leader like this. Revealed like this. "How could you, Elvid? I trusted you!" Nathalya cried out, her face shattered. Elvid shook his head. For a minute, Nathalya believed that she was getting through to him. That he wouldn't turn her in.

"Sometimes, Daddy's love is tough love," Elvid said instead. Then he turned and walked out of her room. She could hear him returning to his other life, the one with his wife and kiddo. And the status it brought.

Nathalya knew she had to act fast. The last Caltrain from the 4th & Townsend depot in San Francisco would be pulling into the California Avenue station soon. She had 5 minutes. Tops.

She ran naked. Past the Baptist Church, across the

sparse traffic on Alma and on towards the rail level crossing (a few hundred yards away from the station).

A part of her was not surprised to see Margarita standing there, her body seemingly rejuvenated after the explosion. Except, it was different this time. It wasn't as solid. More ethereal. Nathalya could see Margarita's skull peeking out from the side of her Versace scarf (a scarf that Elvid had bought for her).

Rain began to fall. It landed slowly on the train tracks. The rhythm was soft at first but then increased in frequency. Tapur, tupur. Nathalya got closer to the train tracks. She laughed as she saw a sign reading: No Shoulder. That's exactly what Margarita looked like to her; a body holding a head. Like a shopper coming out of Whole Foods with a bag of overpriced, organic food.

She heard Margarita laugh, too. *It's just your imagination, Nathalya.*

There's no such thing as ghosts. Especially in the middle of Palo Alto, the technology capital of Silicon Valley.

"Come! Join me, Nathalya! We will be together. Forever!" The voice said. Nathalya looked towards the voice. The appearance of the thing that called itself Margarita had changed. Margarita's formerly perky, 42 D breasts were like old punching bags that sagged to her knees.

Nathalya fancied that she could tell that Margarita had been waiting for her. It was time to go home. But, did she really want to? Did she have any other choice? If she was going to go out, she would do it her way. Nathalia opened her phone and started typing a status update on TSN. It seemed like the body arranging artist, formerly known as Margarita, extended her bony fingers to touch the screen of Nathalya's phone.

The Caltrain was several hundred feet away and getting closer.

Nathalya put her head down on the train tracks. She listened to the sound of the rain. With her eyes closed, it seemed like she was back home in Germany. On the bed. Waiting for Daddy dearest.

"Nathalya," The voice crooned, "I am waiting for you in hell with my smelly, fish taco, Mexican pussy." Margarita's ghost chuckled, giggled and snorted through its skeletal nose.

Nathalya's head rested steadily on the stainless steel rail. The Caltrain was about 50 feet away and Nathalya started laughing about the "No Shoulder" sign again. If she were lucky, and the train hit her the right away, she might be left with no shoulder. The thought made her giggle.

She typed as she waited for the train to hit her.

Nathalya Hitler's Status: **I did my best trying to save Margarita. But it was Elvid's fault. He was raping her. He raped me, too. He told me to keep his semen inside of me, always. He wanted me to give him another baby. I can't bear to think that I am pregnant. I must leave this bitter world now.**

Right before the train hit Nathalya, she saw Gunther clearly. He looked happier, save for the blood and organs around his neck (which looked like a stump). His head was bobbing on his torso and he looked like a zombie bobblehead doll. From that popular show. Walking Zombies.

Nathalya knew that her status update on TSN would teach Elvid a lesson. The motherchucker. No fuck chucker. Elvid is a fucker. A motherfucker.

Nathalya was proud that she could choose her way out. End her life on her terms. Ariba, ariba.

Elvid saw the status update and freaked. He ran outside and hopped into his car. He drove faster than sin toward the train station. By the time he reached it, the last Caltrain had methodically sliced Nathalya's head off. He got out of the car and left it running. He saw that her head had rolled past the tennis courts, the football fields and the field hockey greens. It rested in the parking lot of Palo Alto High School, next to a pile of dog doo.

vii

Elvid, with Nathalya's blood spattered cell phone in hand, sprinted back to his purple Testicla (a hybrid electric truck). He had parked next to the tennis courts and kitty corner from the Town & Country (a prosaic strip mall masquerading as a high end chichi "holistic shopping experience" where nannies and their boys ate $9 cupcakes while sipping $19 organic, vegan, coffee drinks with fancy Italian names). It was about a 9 minute walk, 4 minute sprint, or 2 minute drive from the railroad crossing at Winston Churchill Chateau and Lavender Alma Street.

He calculated that the 1:01 AM (the last train out of the San Francisco Caltrain depot in SOMA, an urban neighborhood as different from Palo Alto as Nikki Minaj is from Katy Perry) nicknamed "The Drunken Bullet" (because of all the nannies in miniskirts sans pink, lacy Victoria's Secret Panties, coming back from clubbing and raving) must have hit (hah! Nathalya lost her head) the California Avenue station in Palo Alto around 2:02 AM.

Elvid figured that the police from downtown Palo Alto were at least 12 minutes away, because they spent most of their time at this hour on the east edge of Palo Alto, near 101. The police pulled over and harassed the (mostly) Black and Hispanic 20's, 30's, and sometimes 40's to 50's guys coming back from nanny sex pursuits in posh Palo Alto places.

Conservative republicans argued that, statistically, more blacks and hispanics were pulled over because the population of East Palo Alto disproportionately skewed that way. Their cars were older models, with rust, dents, softly decaying fading paint jobs and tires on their last treads.

The cops especially liked pulling over nannies in 2013. They would ask the nannies to step out of their cars (the nannies were usually wearing miniskirts that hung just a few inches above their creamy, milky, inner thighs) so the cops could catch a quick glimpse of their crotches. Or get a phone number for a nanny sexting buddy, who would give an occasional blowjob in the back of a squad car. Or so they could take a sexy selfie to post on TSN with a pretty, Polish nanny. The nannies in return could drink and drive with impunity. Sex and sugar used to solve a lot of problems in 2013.

There was a darkness on the edge of town that Elvid had been running from since his youth in the Israeli army. He was determined to outrun the evil. The money from selling his post-IPO stock options in TSN would solve any of his problems. Elvid figured 12 minutes would give him plenty of time to head west on Highway 280 and make a pit stop at Point Lookout (he had had carefree, innocent sex with Nathalya there, once). He could then toss Nathalya's phone (with incriminating pictures of them fucking and sucking) into the Pleasanton Lake (it hugged the highway on the 37 mile jaunt up to San Francisco).

In 2013, during the day, Point Lookout was a cruising spot for gay and, "I am straight but like to cruise the 'Men For Men' section on Craigslist to get some cock here and there, so I must be straight," men. Elvid pulled into the lookout parking lot. It was empty. There was not a living soul there, except Elvid.

Soon, even that would change.

The parking lot sat on a postage stamp sized rectangular lot surrounded by a flimsy, 3 foot tall, aluminum fence. A 60 degree slope became a 90 degree drop down. With an elevation of 1,776 feet (the height of the new World Trade Center in lower Manhattan).

Elvid's car automatically sensed the flimsy fence 69 feet away and applied the brakes. *Worth every penny of the $79,920, this fucking Testicla car*, Elvid thought. *Money does buy you safety.*

Elvid sighed with a mixture of irritation, relief and sorrow. He was sorry that Nathalya had killed herself. She was a great fuck. But he had to protect his status in Palo Alto. She was just a 21-year-old glorified whore with no money. Elvid had status because he had the right car and lots of money. Money can't buy you love, but it sure as hell could buy you status in 2013. And gain access to the vapid vaginas of nonsense nannies. Elvid giggled like Nathalya used to do when she stuck dildos up his ass while cross-dressing in a man's suit.

"Spare me the lies, fucker. You pushed me over the edge, to my death."

Elvid heard Nathalya's voice in his head. But, that was impossible! She was dead! *It's just some loons. They exist here, in California, as well. There's nothing to be afraid of. Be brave, you motherchucker.*

"Ha ha, you motherchucker! You want my pussy? Lick my large labia! Come and get it! Ariba, Ariba! Party time!"

Nathalya's voice seemed closer to him. *It's just loons*, Elvid told himself. He thought of some of her threads on TSN. *Nathalya would never hurt you, Elvid. Remember her posts about unconditional love?*

Nonetheless, Elvid had to work fast. The clock was ticking. The temperature was getting hotter than hell for Elvid. Elvid shrugged that thought off with a devil may care attitude and pulled Nathalya's phone out of his pocket. It was still on TSN. You could never escape TSN in 2013. TSN loved you and you loved TSN.

Elvid uploaded the photograph of Nathalya and him in happier times to TSN.

Nathalya Hitler's Status: **Unconditional love never dies**

Elvid had created an alibi for himself on her phone, he thought. He didn't know Nathalya had his semen trapped in her vaginal cavity. The police would find it and know he had been raping her. Still in his car, he put the phone in his left hand and used the same motion he had when Nathalya and he played frisbee at Dolores park. The phone flew through the air. It seemed like it gained altitude as it made its way over the flimsy fence. Then, swoosh! It dropped into the darkness of the 1,776 foot drop.

Gone! It's over! Freedom, bitches! Elvid rejoiced in his head. Then he felt a cold chill run up his spine.

He felt that Nathalya was closer than ever before. But that was crazy. Irrational. He would drive to San Francisco, get a nice hotel room and text the Nannyluv

Agency to send him another nanny, pronto. He imagined delicate arms and an angelic face, sleek long legs and killer abs. *Yes, Siree, Bob. Some more prime, USDA Grade A pussy!*

Elvid put his car into reverse and hit the gas, but it moved forward, instead. *What the fuck! Testiclas never malfunction!* The car was moving toward the flimsy fence, only 20 feet away from the edge. *Nathalya, you cunt!* Elvid screamed inside.

Then he saw her. Nathalya was on the front seat next to him. She held her detached head in her hands. The false blue eye was gone, the eye socket empty and gaping red. Her blonde hair was matted with blood. Her thighs were open and he could see his semen trickling whitely down her legs.

The Testicla sliced through the fence like Elvid used to glide into Nathalya while sucking her tits. It dangled over the edge then tipped. It was ready to march the 1,776 feet down to freedom.

What you paid for is what you owned in 2013. And, sooner rather than later, on a moonlit San Francisco Bay Area night, what you paid for would come back to you. To haunt you. Elvid heard Nathalya (IT?) very clearly. Nathalya's voice was grating to the ears; it was full of gravel and dirt from the railroad tracks and the level crossing.

"Daddy," IT said.

THE
END

AUTHOR'S ACKNOWLEDGEMENTS

To every person who has contributed to my life in any way, shape or form: thank you. To all of my faithful readers throughout this process: MANY THANKS!

To all Quorans, your inspiration has been invaluable (users from www.Quora.com). Thank you all.

Thanks especially to Princessthecat.

Special thanks to Edgar Allen Poe (he can still read after death). Thanks to the 100 billion authors who have come before me.

Most of all, thanks to the technology. Because of you, I could self-publish this with relative ease. I heard the Internet was going to be big. And here's tangible proof.

JULIE PRENTICE

Julie Prentice is a Dartmouth College alumna.

She lives and grew up only an hour away from the College on the Hill in picturesque Montpelier, the capital of Vermont.

This is her first published work.

Julie is working on her first novel and a compilation of stories about life in a unique, quintessential piece of America, Montpeculier.

Check out this rising asteroid at:
http://www.julieprentice.com

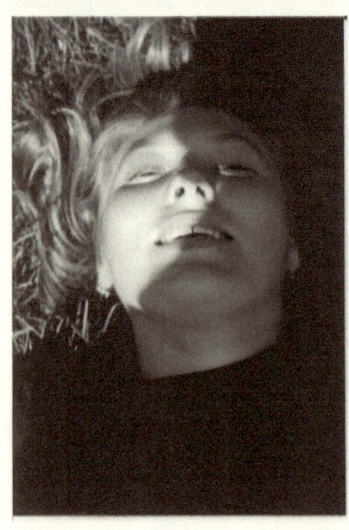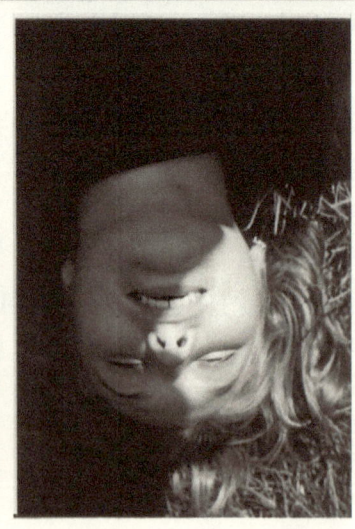

www.ingramcontent.com/pod-product-compliance
Lightning Source LLC
Chambersburg PA
CBHW020619150626
46552CB00026B/1944